The
PARTY WALL ACT
Explained

A Commentary on the Party Wall etc. Act 1996

Second Edition

Promoting excellence
in party wall practice

THE PYRAMUS & THISBE CLUB
Website - www.partywalls.org.uk
Email - info@partywalls.org.uk

The Pyramus & Thisbe Club (named after the two lovers separated by a wall in Shakespeare's *A Midsummer Night's Dream "The Wall is down that parted their fathers"*) was founded in 1974 as a forum for discussion on all matters in connection with party walls.

The Club has been addressed by historic surveyors, The City (of London) Solicitor, barristers, judges, engineers and its own members. An Official Referee has even conducted a mock hearing to decide a controversial issue and, although his finding does not have the force of law, his ruling that you may raise on a cantilever has been widely accepted.

The only qualification for membership is a serious professional interest in the subject and a willingness to disseminate information among one's fellow members about difficult or interesting cases. The Royal Institution of Chartered Surveyors, or the publishers, will put any enquirers in touch with the current Chairman or membership secretary.

ISBN 978-0-9558454-0-6
Published by
The Pyramus & Thisbe Club

from
Administration Office
Rathdale House, 30 Back Road
Rathfriland, Co Down
BT34 5QF

Printed in the UK by
Commercial Graphics Limited

CONTENTS

FOREWARD

by

The Lord Dubs

When the Party Wall Bill came up for debate in the House of Lords, I was given a copy of The Pyramus & Thisbe Club's original *Green Book*, so that I could understand the background of the London Building Acts on which the Bill was based. I was pleased to discover a remarkably clear exposition of the clauses of the Act, set out in such a way as to make it plain what was well established law, what was precedent and what might be done to improve it.

I was moved to say during the debate that, *"I do not think I have ever come across such a clear explanation of legislation...the book is a model of clarity. It would be nice if Government Departments were to consider the book to determine how they could emulate this clear approach to explaining legislation."*

The Bill, which has now become the Party Wall etc Act 1996, tried to incorporate as many as possible of the ideas for improvement from the *Green Book*. This new publication, therefore, does not have any such suggestions, but retains the clear-cut division between *Interpretation* and *Comment*, which was so helpful in the earlier version. I congratulate the authors, and commend the book to anyone who wants a better understanding of the legislation. I also congratulate Lord Lytton for his Bill and for getting it through Parliament.

THE PROLOGUE

The Party Wall etc Act 1996 extends legislation and procedures well established in London to the whole of England and Wales. This latest annotated version of the Act is a successor to the similar commentary on the London Building Acts, produced in 1993 by The Pyramus & Thisbe Club, a society of people interested in party wall matters, and currently numbering approx 1,000 members. The earlier "Green Book" was the result of many hours of study by a Working Party of the Club to produce an interim report, which was carefully criticised by the existing membership, and then edited into a final version.

The 1993 book contained many suggestions for improving the legislation, and on 23 November 1995 a Private Bill was introduced in the House of Lords by the Earl of Lytton, who had taken over as a sponsor from Lord Lucas of Crudwell. Sir Sydney Chapman saw the Bill safely through the Commons, and in July 1996 the Act received the Royal Assent.

This is the second revised version of the "Green Book" which deals with the Party Wall etc Act 1996. The first was published in 1996 and was produced by the most eminent of party wall surveyors of the day, the late John Anstey, Eric Roe and Donald Ensom, along with the Earl of Lytton, who did so much to promote the Party Wall Bill.

The Act has now been with us countrywide for over 10 years and it was felt an updated version should be published. A new Working Party, consisting of Graham North (Chairman), Aidan Cosgrave, Clive Carlile, Donald Jessop and Alex Schatunowski, was formed for this purpose, assisted on the legal nuances by Andrew Smith.

Members views, opinions and experiences were sought as the Act spread across England and Wales and this book tries to deal with the most relevant and common issues which arise when administering the legislation.

INTRODUCTION
The Party Wall etc Act 1996

This Act provides owners of buildings with certain new rights and obligations to other owners in relation to party walls and similar structures. At the same time it provides a framework for a disciplined approach to exercising these rights. These matters are generally dealt with under Sections 1 to 5.

Important definitions are to be found in Section 20. These should be read and understood before considering this commentary.

Section 6 introduces obligations on anyone digging an excavation near another owner's building. Notices must be served and procedures followed.

There are provisions for compensation, for rights of entry and for the safeguarding of some existing easements.

The Act lays down strict procedures for the resolution of disputes and these are in Sections 10 to 14. They provide for the appointment of a surveyor or surveyors who have the power to sort out problems.

Later sections deal with the usual miscellaneous matters in an Act, including the fact that it may be an offence to step outside the Act's provisions.

Where a surveyor or owner is referred as "he", it means "she" as well. The decision, taken after consultation with several female building surveyors, is also consistent with the standard legal terminology of the Act.

List of sections

Party Wall etc Act 1996

ARRANGEMENT OF SECTIONS

Expenses

Miscellaneous

General

Party Wall etc Act 1996

An Act to make provision in respect of party walls, and excavation and construction in proximity to certain buildings or structures; and for connected purposes.

COMMENT:
*The word "etc" in the title (derived from the Latin **et cetera**, literally meaning "and the rest") refers to those provisions of the Act which deal with matters such as adjacent excavation, which are not strictly to do with party walls.*

New building on line of junction
s.1(1)(a)&(b)

Construction and repair of walls on line of junction

1.- (1) This section shall have effect where lands of different owners adjoin and –

    (a) are not built on at the line of junction; or

    (b) are built on at the line of junction only to the extent of a boundary wall (not being a party fence wall or the external wall of a building),

and either owner is about to build on any part of the line of junction.

INTERPRETATION
This section regulates proposals to construct walls either at or astride the legal boundary between owners (known as the line of junction), where there exists at present no wall at all, or only a boundary wall wholly on one owner's land and belonging solely to that owner.

COMMENT
In that case, if either owner wants to 'build' at or astride the line of junction, he follows the procedures set out in the subsections below.

Section 1 does not apply if there is an existing building at the line of junction.

(2) If a building owner desires to build a party wall or party fence wall on the line of junction he shall, at least one month before he intends the building work to start, serve on any adjoining owner a notice which indicates his desire to build and describes the intended wall.

INTERPRETATION

This type of wall, above ground, would stand astride the line of junction, and therefore on the land of two owners (see the definitions for a party fence wall and party wall in s.20). Of itself, projection of footings across the boundary (where the wall itself is on one owner's side only), does not make the structure "party".

COMMENT
One month is one calendar month.

(3) If, having been served with notice described in subsection (2), an adjoining owner serves on the building owner a notice indicating his consent to the building of a party wall or party fence wall –

(a) the wall shall be built half on the land of each of the two owners or in such other position as may be agreed between the two owners; and

(b) the expense of building the wall shall be from time to time defrayed by the two owners in such proportion as has regard to the use made or to be made of the wall by each of them and to the cost of labour and materials prevailing at the time when that use is made by each owner respectively.

INTERPRETATION
Having received a notice, the adjoining owner may agree to the proposal, in which case the parties can also agree exactly where the wall will be placed in relation to the boundary and how it shall be paid for, according to the use to be made of it by each owner. See subsection (4) for what happens if the adjoining owner does not consent.

COMMENT
If both owners want a party wall, it is likely to be built half on each side of the boundary, but paragraph (b) envisages that one owner may make more use of the wall at the time of its construction than the other. Payment for the wall relates to the use for which it is being built, not its position.

(4) If, having been served with notice described in subsection (2), an adjoining owner does not consent under this subsection to the building of a party wall or party fence wall, the building owner may only build the wall –

(a) at his own expense; and

(b) as an external wall or a fence wall, as the case may be, placed wholly on his own land,

and consent under this subsection is consent by a notice served within the period of fourteen days beginning with the day on which the notice described in subsection (2) is served.

INTERPRETATION
If the adjoining owner does not consent positively within 14 days, the building owner cannot build a party wall astride the boundary, and thus, where one does not already exist, a party wall cannot be forced on an adjoining owner. In that case, any wall which the building owner constructs on his own land, at his own expense, will not be "party".

COMMENT
Lest the adjoining owner's failure to consent should cause the building owner to serve a further notice, and thus suffer delay, he would be well advised to serve at the outset under both subsections (2) and (5) as alternatives, using two separate forms of notice.

Absence of consent does not deem a statutory dissent for the purpose of subsection (8).

(5) If the building owner desires to build on the line of junction a wall placed wholly on his own land he shall, at least one month before he intends the building work to start, serve on any adjoining owner a notice which indicates his desire to build and describes the intended wall.

INTERPRETATION
This subsection is to protect the adjoining owner from unannounced works that could affect the legal demarcation and/or the stability of his land.

COMMENT
There should rarely be any need for a "dispute" about this kind of wall. If any, it will be about where the wall is placed in relation to the boundary.

The Working Party was unable to agree unanimously as to whether a building owner may enter an adjoining owner's land under s.8 (rights of entry) to build a wall above ground having served notice under s.1(5). It hinges on the interpretation of the phrase "work in pursuance of this Act" cited in s.8. There are three views within The Working Party as follows:

View 1:   *The majority view is that the building owner may enter and remain on adjoining land in order to build such a wall. He may do so upon the expiration of the one month and 14-day notice periods under s.1 and s.8 respectively unless an actual dispute arises, in which case the matter must first be determined by surveyors appointed under s.10.*

s.1(5)(continued)

Reasoning: *Work undertaken as described in a notice served pursuant to s.1(5) is "work in pursuance of the Act". The building owner may therefore enter the adjoining land, subject to serving notice of entry under s.8*
Access must not cause the adjoining owner unnecessary inconvenience and the adjoining owner is entitled to compensation for any damage to his property under s.1(7)(a) and for damage and loss as set out in s.7(2).

View 2: *A second view, which differs slightly from the first, is that the building owner may only enter the adjoining land if the adjoining owner consents or if an actual dispute arises. In the event of a dispute the appointed surveyors would determine whether the need for access is connected to, and necessary for, the building of the wall and make their award accordingly. In the absence of consent or an award, such as might happen if an adjoining owner does not respond to the notice, the building owner may not enter the adjoining owner's land.*

Reasoning: *The details of the work must be settled either by the owners or in accordance with s.10 before it can be considered to be "work in pursuance of the Act".*

View 3   *A third view is that a building owner does not have a right to enter an adjoining owner's land under s.8 for the purposes of building such a wall.*

Reasoning: *"Work in pursuance of this Act" means work in exercise of the authority conferred by the Act. The Act does not confer authority to build a wall wholly on a building owner's land: he is entitled to do this anyway without the sanction of the Act (compare this with s.2 where the Act confers rights to raise a party wall, which would otherwise be a trespass.) A wall built under s.1(5) is therefore not "work in pursuance of the Act" and s.8 (rights of entry) does not apply.*

The Act simply requires the building owner to notify the adjoining owner before building at the line of junction so that the adjoining owner is given an opportunity to dispute the position of the intended wall and for the dispute to be determined by surveyors in accordance with s.10. If an adjoining owner does not respond to a s.1(5) notice the building owner can proceed to build the wall after the expiration of the one-month period but he may not enter any adjoining land without the express consent of the owner of that land.

In one case concerning an appeal to a third surveyor's award a county court judgement held that a building owner did not have a right of entry onto an adjoining owner's land under s.8 for building a wall on the line of junction and entirely on his own land. The building owner chose to have no legal representation in the case and the decision was not appealed and is not legal precedent.

Whatever a surveyor's own view may be on whether a right of entry may be claimed, he would be well advised to make his appointing owner aware of the differing views.

The Working Party agreed unanimously that a building owner would be entitled to access onto the adjoining owner's land under s.8 to project foundations onto next door's land as described in s.1(6) or if a party wall or party fence wall is built as set out in s.1(2) and 1(3).

(6) Where the building owner builds a wall wholly on his own land in accordance with subsection (4) or (5) he shall have the right, at any time in the period which –

(a) begins one month after the day on which the notice mentioned in the subsection concerned was served, and

(b) ends twelve months after that day,

to place below the level of the land of the adjoining owner such projecting footings and foundations as are necessary for the construction of the wall.

INTERPRETATION
A building owner building a wall on his land, on (but not astride) the boundary may place footings or foundations necessary for its construction, on the land of the adjoining owner.

COMMENT
There is some scope for dispute as to what extent of projection is necessary for the construction of the wall. An adjoining owner cannot simply refuse to allow projecting footings below ground. See also s.2(2)(g) for the right of the adjoining owner subsequently to cut off such projections if necessary. However, there is no right for the building owner (as he will be then) to recover the costs of doing so.

"Special foundations" (see s.7(4) and definition in s.20) are not permitted without express consent.

(7) Where the building owner builds a wall wholly on his own land in accordance with subsection (4) or (5) he shall do so at his own expense and shall compensate any adjoining owner and any adjoining occupier for any damage to his property occasioned by –

(a) the building of the wall;

(b) the placing of any footings or foundations placed in accordance with subsection (6).

INTERPRETATION
When a wall is built under subsections (4) or (5), the building owner must pay for its construction and must pay compensation for any damage which its construction causes, for example to flowerbeds, driveways, drains or other underground services.

COMMENT
It may be prudent for the building owner to record the condition of the adjoining owner's land before works proceed to obviate the possibility of a dispute about damage arising.

s.1(8)

(8) Where any dispute arises under this section between the building owner and any adjoining owner or occupier it is to be determined in accordance with section 10.

INTERPRETATION
For example, a disagreement as to the necessary projection of footings could be referred to surveyors appointed under s.10. An award could be produced to settle any such dispute, or perhaps a dispute about the compensation for damage.

COMMENT
Any dispute in this context means an actual dispute. There is no "deemed" dispute under section 1 and the surveyors appointed to determine any dispute under this section may award costs according with the cause and event.

2. – (1) This section applies where lands of different owners adjoin and at the line of junction the said lands are built on or a boundary wall, being a party fence wall or the external wall of a building, has been erected.

INTERPRETATION
This section confers important rights on owners in respect of walls on or astride the legal boundary line (other than those dealt with in s.1). These may be party fence walls (such as a garden wall), party walls (separating buildings), or the external wall of one owner's building. Definitions of party wall and party fence wall are given in s.20.

COMMENT
It should be noted that these rights do not override the need for planning permission, building regulation approval or listed building consent. The Act also does not override rights of light to neighbouring windows. This section confers the right to affect certain rights which have the characteristics of easements, but see s.9 for those which cannot be overridden. Actions under this section are likely, in general, to be the most common subject of party wall procedures, and the various rights and obligations are set out in detail in the following subsections.

(2) A building owner shall have the following rights –

    (a) to underpin, thicken or raise a party structure, a party fence wall, or an external wall which belongs to the building owner and it is built against a party structure or party fence wall;

INTERPRETATION
Paragraph (a) allows the underpinning, thickening, or raising of either a party structure or an external wall built against a party structure. Subsection (3) makes it clear that this right is only exercisable provided that the building owner makes good any damage to the adjoining owner's premises, (including furnishings) and carries up (ie. extends upwards or outwards) as necessary any chimneys of the adjoining property, in order that they will continue to function effectively.

COMMENT

This means, for example, that if subsidence requires the underpinning of a property, the whole thickness of the party wall may be underpinned. If a building owner wants to create a loft extension, he may raise the whole thickness of the party wall at roof level.

"Raising" has been held to include extending downwards, and a strong body of opinion believes that it also includes raising on a cantilever. In the downwards case, reinforcing would count as special foundations, and would not be permitted without express consent.

Where underpinning is proposed because of defect or want of repair, the owners or surveyors must apportion the cost of the work in accordance with section 11(4).

(b) to make good, repair or demolish and rebuild, a party structure or party fence wall in a case where such work is necessary on account of defect or want of repair of the structure or wall;

INTERPRETATION

Where a wall needs repair, this allows an owner to carry out such repair, including, if necessary, the right to demolish and rebuild a defective party structure.

COMMENT

It is important to note that responsibility for costs differs depending on whether work is carried out because a wall is in disrepair or because the wall does not suit the building owner's purposes. The adjoining owner may well be called upon to contribute to the cost in the former case, but not in the latter (see s.11(5)).

(c) to demolish a partition which separates buildings belonging to different owners but does not conform with statutory requirements and to build instead a party wall which does so conform;

(d) in the case of buildings connected by arches or structures over public ways or over passages belonging to other persons, to demolish the whole or part of such buildings, arches or structures which do not conform with statutory requirements and to rebuild them so that they do so conform;

INTERPRETATION

Paragraph (c) allows a partition between buildings which does not comply with prevailing statutory requirements, for example with current building regulations, to be rebuilt to comply with those regulations.

The following paragraph (d), allows the rebuilding of structures carried on arches over pubic ways or passageways in third party ownership, in order to make them conform to statutory requirements.

COMMENT

Both these paragraphs are little used, especially since subsection (8) confers deemed conformity on many otherwise non-conforming structures. However, these paragraphs make clear a building owner's right to rebuild in conformity if he wishes to do so, at his own cost.

Note that defect on account of non-conformity can only arise post 1996.

(e) to demolish a party structure which is of insufficient strength or height for the purposes of any intended building of the building owner and to rebuild it of sufficient strength or height for the said purposes (including rebuilding to a lesser height or thickness where the rebuilt structure is of sufficient strength and height for the purposes of any adjoining owner);

INTERPRETATION
The building owner may take down a party structure which is not strong enough or high enough for his purposes, and rebuild it so that it is adequate. Subsection (4) stated that this right is only exercisable provided that he makes good any damage and rebuilds any chimneys to an agreed height.

The building owner also has the right to take down (temporarily) a wall of which the adjoining owner is making full use, but in that case he has to comply with s.7(3) by providing adequate protection, and making good fully afterwards in accordance with s.2(4) and paying a fair allowance for disturbance and inconvenience in accordance with section 11(6).

The costs of such an operation can be very considerable, and should not be lightly undertaken.

COMMENT
When a party structure is to be rebuilt to a lesser thickness, it should be built half on the land of each of the two owners or in such other position as may be agreed by the two owners.

(f) to cut into a party structure for any purpose (which may be or include the purpose of inserting a damp proof course);

INTERPRETATION

This paragraph gives the right to cut into a party structure (usually to insert a beam, or to bond in a wall, but it could also include the insertion of flashings) and specifically includes the right to insert a damp proof course, subject, to making good any damage which this may cause to the adjoining owner's premises under subsection (5). It does not give the right to cut an opening for a door, window or vent.

COMMENT

The formation of any permanent opening in a party structure is not covered by the Act and may only proceed with the express consent of the owners.

The injection of a chemical damp proof course would require a notice under this subsection.

(g) to cut away from a party wall, party fence wall, external wall or boundary wall any footing or any projecting chimney breast, jamb or flue, or other projection on or over the land of the building owner in order to erect, raise or underpin any such wall or for any other purpose;

INTERPRETATION
This paragraph allows the building owner to cut away any projections, such as footings or chimney breasts, which are on or over his land, in order that he can raise, build or underpin a wall on the boundary, subject to making good any damage, in this case under subsection (5).

COMMENT
Clearly such cutting off may not be carried out in such a way as to destroy the effectiveness of any flues, which may have to be reinstated in the rebuilding, even if in a different form. Nor may any other work be executed in contravention of good building practice or regulatory requirements as described in section 7(5)(a).

(h) to cut away or demolish parts of any wall or building of an adjoining owner overhanging the land of the building owner or overhanging a party wall, to the extent that it is necessary to cut away or demolish the parts to enable a vertical wall to be erected or raised against the wall or building of the adjoining owner;

INTERPRETATION
A building owner may cut off projections, such as gutters or eaves, when they overhang either the land (including the building) of the building owner, or the party wall, if this is necessary in order to allow the party wall to be raised, or an external wall to be erected. Any drainage problems which this creates must be resolved by the building owner under his duty to make good damage, prescribed in subsection (5).

COMMENT
The mere fact that a gutter overhangs either the party wall or the building owner's land cannot prevent the building owner from raising a wall. Once again, proper standards of workmanship and regulatory compliance continue to apply.

(j)   to cut into the wall of an adjoining owner's building in order to insert a flashing or other weather-proofing of a wall erected against that wall;

INTERPRETATION

Although s.2(2)(f) gives a right to cut into a party wall for a flashing, often a building owner will be raising an independent building, abutting another wall or building, and it is in both parties' interests that the junction should be weatherproofed or flashed. This paragraph gives that right.

COMMENT

Any damage to the adjoining owner's wall must be made good under subsection (6).

Note that this paragraph does not permit a building owner to dress a flashing over the lower parapet wall of an adjoining owner, unless it is cut into the parapet wall.

(k) to execute any other necessary works incidental to the connection of a party structure with the premises adjoining it;

INTERPRETATION

This paragraph relates to tying party walls to buildings either side of them, and can be used to unite an old party wall with the new building of the building owner, or to tie the party wall more firmly to the adjoining owner's building when the building owner's premises are demolished. It also allows a party wall to be tied to an independent building abutting it.

(l) to raise a party fence wall, or to raise such a wall for use as a party wall, and to demolish a party fence wall and rebuild it as a party fence wall or as a party wall;

INTERPRETATION

This right to demolish and rebuild can also change the nature of a wall from a party fence wall to a party wall. Since a wall astride a boundary with a building on one side only is a party wall, this paragraph makes it clear that a garden wall, if it is a party fence wall, may be demolished and rebuilt (astride the boundary) to enclose a building.

COMMENT
In all circumstances the cost of such work would be met by the building owner who wanted the wall also to serve his new building in accordance with section 11(1).

If a party fence wall is already less than 2 metres in height, then the requirement to rebuild means to a height no less than its existing height.

s.2(2)(m)

(m) subject to the provisions of section 11(7), to reduce, or to demolish and rebuild, a party wall or party fence wall to –

    (i) a height of not less than two metres where the wall is not used by an adjoining owner to any greater extent than a boundary wall; or

    (ii) a height currently enclosed upon by the building of an adjoining owner;

INTERPRETATION

Where a party wall or party fence wall is too high for the new purposes of one owner only, he can reduce it to a minimum height of two metres, or the height of an adjoining building. For example, one owner may use a wall astride the boundary to enclose a high building, while the adjoining owner may only need a garden wall. The first owner, too, now only wants a garden wall, and is bound to leave it two metres high, measured from the adjoining owner's land. However, if the adjoining owner has a building using the wall, the building owner may only reduce the wall to such a height as encloses the adjoining owner's existing building, plus a parapet to satisfy building or fire regulations if necessary, as prescribed by subsection (7).

COMMENT

If both parties wished to remove the wall completely, this could be done by agreement. This paragraph merely imposes minimum heights which must be respected by the building owner if required by the adjoining owner.

If the adjoining owner could prove that he had paid for a greater height than two metres at an earlier date, he could insist on the retention of the wall at that height.

In the exercise of this right, there are counter notice provisions under section 4 which are extended under section 11(7) and an adjoining owner may elect to have so much of the party wall as it wishes retained above that proposed to be removed, subject to the adjoining owner paying for the cost of the retained section.

(n) to expose a party wall or party structure hitherto enclosed subject to providing adequate weathering.

INTERPRETATION

A building owner may demolish all or part of his building, exposing the party wall to the elements, either temporarily or permanently, as long as he provides suitable protection for the wall.

COMMENT

"Adequate" will depend upon the length of time that the wall is likely to remain exposed, and could vary from felt and battens to permanent rendering. In some cases no protection at all may be necessary.

(3) Where work mentioned in paragraph (a) of subsection (2) is not necessary on account of defect or want of repair of the structure or wall concerned, the right falling within that paragraph is exercisable –

(a) subject to making good all damage occasioned by the work to the adjoining premises or to their internal furnishings and decorations; and

(b) where the work is to a party structure or external wall, subject to carrying any relevant flues and chimney stacks up to such a height and in such materials as may be agreed between the building owner and the adjoining owner concerned or, in the event of dispute, determined in accordance with section 10;

and relevant flues and chimney stacks are those, which belong to the adjoining owner and either form part of or rest on or against the party structure or external wall.

(4) The right falling within subsection (2)(e) is exercisable subject to-

(a) making good all damage occasioned by the work to the adjoining premises or to their internal furnishings and decorations; and

(b) carrying any relevant flues and chimney stacks up to such a height and in such materials as may be agreed between the building owner and the adjoining owner concerned or, in the event of dispute, determined in accordance with section 10.

and relevant flues and chimney stacks are those which belong to an adjoining owner and either form part of or rest on or against the party structure.

INTERPRETATION

These subsections apply when work under paragraphs (a) or (e) of subsection (2) of s.2 is not made necessary by defect but is being carried out for the building owner's purposes. In those cases he is liable for all the making good necessary to next door's premises and, if required to do so by the adjoining owner, he has to carry up any flues so that they will continue to be effective.

COMMENT

Very often, the adjoining owner will be quite happy to see disused flues capped and vented. The flues may have to be taken down temporarily and then rebuilt where a party wall is being demolished and rebuilt under s.2 (2)(e). Any dispute as to raising is referred to the appointed surveyors. Where there is defect or a repair is necessary then section 11(4) will apply which provides for an apportionment of costs between the parties.

(5) Any right falling within subsection (2)(f), (g) or (h) is exercisable subject to making good all damage occasioned by the work to the adjoining premises or to their internal furnishings and decorations.

INTERPRETATION

When a building owner cuts into the party structure, or cuts off any projecting parts of an adjoining building under the paragraphs cited, he is liable to make good any damage, which his works cause.

(6) The right falling within subsection (2)(j) is exercisable subject to making good all damage occasioned by the work to the wall of the adjoining owner's building.

INTERPRETATION
If inserting a flashing causes any damage, the building owner must make it good.

COMMENT
In contrast with subsection (3), (4) and (5), this subsection excludes internal furnishings and decorations, but see s.7 (1) and (2).

(7)   The right falling within subsection (2)(m) is exercisable subject to –

(a)   reconstructing any parapet or replacing an existing parapet with another one; or

(b)   constructing a parapet where one is needed but did not exist before.

INTERPRETATION
When reducing the height of a party wall, or rebuilding one to a lesser height, under s.2(2)(e) and (m), there may be a need for a parapet above the actual height enclosed on by the adjoining owner. In that case the building owner must provide one.

COMMENT
There is no express requirement where a party wall is reduced in height under s.2(2)(e) to provide a parapet. However, if the owners are in dispute, then it is probable that the appointed surveyors will make an award providing for a parapet as good building practice.

(8) For the purposes of this section a building or structure which was erected before the day on which this Act was passed shall be deemed to conform with statutory requirements if it conforms with the statues regulating buildings or structures on the date on which it was erected.

INTERPRETATION

Subsection (8) provides that, for the purpose of s.2, a structure shall be deemed to have been constructed in accordance with prevailing statutory requirements if it met those in force when it was erected.

COMMENT

There is no need therefore to rebuild a structure under s.2(2)(c) or (d), for example, merely because it no longer conforms to modern building regulations, at least so far as this Act is concerned. You may, however, if you wish to do so, and if other structural reasons make it desirable.

In whatever circumstances, the building owner will be required to meet the whole cost of putting the structure into conformity.

3. - (1) Before exercising any right conferred on him by section 2 a building owner shall serve on any adjoining owner a notice (in this Act referred to as a "party structure notice") stating -

(a) the name and address of the building owner;

(b) the nature and particulars of the proposed work including, in cases where the building owner proposes to construct special foundations, plans, sections and details of construction of the special foundations together with reasonable particulars of the loads to be carried thereby; and

(c) the date on which the proposed work will begin.

INTERPRETATION
A party structure notice must be served before exercising any rights conferred under s.2. An injunction could be granted, *ex parte*, to stop unauthorised works, against the owner or the builder, or even a mandatory (pulling down) injunction against works wholly or partly completed.

Anyone intending to exercise the rights given in s.2 must give notice in writing to all adjoining owners, which would include any owners as defined in s.20 stating the name and address of the building owner, the date on which work will begin, and particulars of the intended work.

s.3(1)(a)(b)&(c) *(continued)*

COMMENT

It is important to ensure that the building owner's name is correctly given, and that all the adjoining ownerships have been identified, even if not all their names are known. The starting date must be at least two months ahead, but could be referred to as "as soon as notice has run".

Since special foundations are not permitted except by express agreement (see s.2.7(4)), full details of any which the building owner would like to construct must be supplied with the notice.

Notifiable work commencing without notice is unlawful and will remain so until regularised between the owners who may elect to appoint surveyors to settle matters in accordance with s.10. Although a statutory notice does not need to be issued to carry out works affecting a means of escape, it is always a good idea to notify anyone likely to be affected, since there may be legal considerations not apparent to the eye.

(2) A party structure notice shall –

    (a) be served at least two months before the date on which the proposed work will begin;

    (b) cease to have effect if the work to which it relates –

        (i) has not begun within the period of twelve months beginning with the day on which the notice is served; and

        (ii) is not prosecuted with due diligence.

INTERPRETATION

A party structure notice must be served at least two months in advance of commencement of the notifiable work but doubts about exact starting times can be avoided by the suggested phase: "as soon as notice has run". If work does not begin for twelve months after notice, and an award has not been made, the notice ceases to have any effect and a new notice must be served.

COMMENT

This subsection avoids an adjoining owner being exposed indefinitely to the prospect of work starting, and also to the unnecessary protraction of building works next door.

If the work starts and then stops for an unreasonable length of time, a new notice must be served unless the works are being carried out under an award in which case the terms of the award will apply.

s.3(3)(a)&(b)

(3) Nothing in this section shall –

(a) prevent a building owner from exercising with the consent in writing of the adjoining owners and of the adjoining occupiers any right conferred on him by section 2; or

(b) require a building owner to serve any party structure notice before complying with any notice served under any statutory provisions relating to dangerous or neglected structure.

INTERPRETATION
A building owner may proceed immediately if he has the written consent of the adjoining owner, or importantly, is complying with a dangerous structure notice or similar statutory notice.

COMMENT
It is important to observe the requirement for written consent. It is not enough to ask a neighbour's consent over the fence or the telephone. If he is misunderstood, or changes his mind later, the purported consent will not satisfy the requirements of the Act. If the adjoining owner consents, and the time of a notice expires, then a fresh notice must be served. If notice is not served, any consent must expressly refer to the work and the starting date. It is believed that the consent would expire after 12 months.

A schedule of condition can be agreed and a building owner may be prepared to meet the reasonable costs of an adjoining owner and/or occupier in its administration as a condition of their consent.

If an adjoining owner does grant consent to the works he shall still have the provisions of the Act to fall back upon in the event of damage or loss arising. In the event of a dispute subsequently arising surveyors shall be appointed in accordance with section s.10 and an award made.

4. - (1) An adjoining owner may, having been served with a party structure notice serve on the building owner a notice (in this Act referred to as a "counter notice") setting out –

(a) in respect of a party fence wall or party structure, a requirement that the building owner build in or on the wall or structure to which the notice relates such chimney copings, breasts, jambs or flues, or such piers or recesses or other like works, as may reasonably be required for the convenience of the adjoining owner;

(b) in respect of special foundations to which the adjoining owner consents under section 7(4) below, a requirement that the special foundations–

(i) be placed at a specified greater depth than that proposed by the building owner; or

(ii) be constructed of sufficient strength to bear the load to be carried by columns of any intended building of the adjoining owner,

or both.

INTERPRETATION

An adjoining owner who has received a notice may serve a counter notice requiring additional works, such as the provision of piers or recesses, or the construction of chimney breasts, etc., to be carried out for his benefit. An adjoining owner may also ask for special foundations to be deeper or stronger than the building owner's original proposal, but in all these cases he will be liable for the additional cost, under s.11(9).

COMMENT

More often, these requirements are settled by the surveyors in the course of negotiating an award, as they are empowered to do by s.10(10) and (12), although it is for the owner to serve the counter notice, not the surveyor unless expressly authorised. In either case, the adjoining owner may be liable for some of the costs under s.11(9).

Refer to s.15 regarding the service of notice.

s.4(2)(a)&(b)

(2) A counter notice shall –

    (a) specify the works required by the notice to be executed and shall be accompanied by plans, sections and particulars of such works; and

    (b) be served within the period of one month beginning with the day on which the party structure notice is served.

INTERPRETATION
A counter notice has to be given within one month after service of the original party structure notice, and must in its turn specify what works are required.

COMMENT
Bear in mind that this section requires the adjoining owner to specifically describe the required works that they wish the building owner to include in the counter notice so as to avoid delaying the building owner unreasonably.

(3) A building owner on whom a counter notice has been served shall comply with the requirements of the counter notice unless the execution of the works required by the counter notice would –

(a) be injurious to him;

(b) cause unnecessary inconvenience to him; or

(c) cause unnecessary delay in the execution of the works pursuant to the party structure notice.

INTERPRETATION
A building owner must comply with a counter notice unless the effect on him would be unreasonable.

COMMENT
Any dispute as to whether a building owner's contentions are justified or correct can be referred to the surveyors appointed under s.10. Costs are a separate matter, dealt with at s.11(9).

5. If an owner on whom a party structure notice or a counter notice has been served does not serve a notice indicating his consent to it within the period of fourteens days beginning with the day on which the party structure notice or counter notice was served, he shall be deemed to have dissented from the notice and a dispute shall be deemed to have arisen between the parties.

INTERPRETATION

To ensure that progress is made after notice is served, and that failure to reply does not hold up that progress, consent must be expressed within fourteen days, otherwise a dispute is deemed to have arisen. The provisions of s.10 will then apply.

COMMENT

It would always be possible for an adjoining owner subsequently to indicate his consent under s.3(3)(a), but his failure to do so within the specified time sets in motion the default procedure of s.10.

6. - (1) This section applies where –

(a) a building owner proposes to excavate, or excavate for and erect a building or structure, within a distance of three metres measured horizontally from any part of a building or structure of an adjoining owner; and

(b) any part of the proposed excavation, building or structure will within those three metres extend to a lower level than the level of the bottom of the foundations of the building or structure of the adjoining owner.

INTERPRETATION
This section places obligations on a building owner who wishes to excavate within certain distances of another owner's building or structure, regardless of the reasons and even if the excavation is later to be filled in. The bottom of a pile is the bottom of the foundation, for either building. However, although an adjoining building may be supported off piles, there may be adjacent boundary walls or other structures standing on the adjoining owner's land and which have shallower foundations. Where any part of these structures are within 3 or 6 metres of the proposed excavation, notice will need to be served. For the purposes of this section "adjoining" means within three metres in s.6(1) and within six metres in s.6(2). See subsection (4).

Notice must be given where the excavation or construction come within the limits shown in the diagram opposite. Note that the minimal distance applies either to the actual structure being built or to the excavation for it.

COMMENT
The necessity for serving notice for a small trial hole or a test bore is not universally agreed. If in doubt, it would seem wise to serve a notice.

A "structure" must have a foundation for it to be a relevant structure under the Act. Therefore, this would not include a timber fence or shed unless it had a concrete base forming the foundation for the shed.

Section 6 deals with proposed excavations. Some of today's ground work techniques may not strictly constitute "excavation" but could destabilise an adjoining owner's building or structure and it would be advisable for a building owner to serve notice.

three metre notice diagram

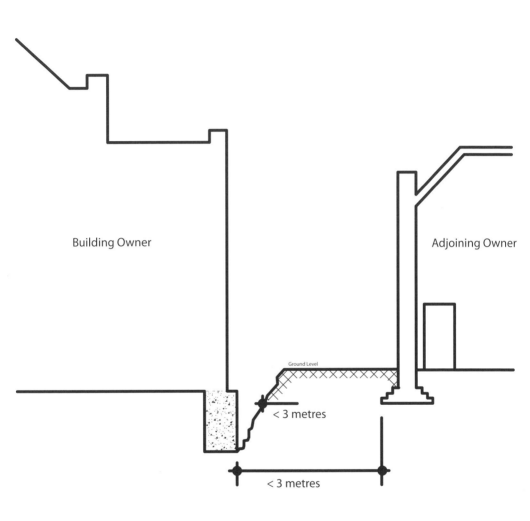

Building Owner

Adjoining Owner

Ground Level

< 3 metres

< 3 metres

Building Owner's excavation or foundations

s.6(2)(a)&(b)

(2) This section also applies where –

    (a) a building owner proposes to excavate, or excavate for and erect a building or structure, within a distance of six metres measured horizontally from any part of a building or structure of an adjoining owner; and

    (b) any part of the proposed excavation, building or structure will within those six metres meet a plane drawn downwards in the direction of the excavation, building or structure of the building owner at an angle of forty-five degrees to the horizontal from the line formed by the intersection of the plane of the level of the bottom of the foundations of the building or structure of the adjoining owner with the plane of the external face of the external wall of the building or structure of the adjoining owner.

INTERPRETATION

Subsection (2) relates to the same activities as (1), but applies when the building owner's actions would cut through a diagonal plane at 45 degrees from where the face of the wall of the adjoining building, projected downwards, would meet the bottom of its foundations, within six metres measured horizontally from nearest part to nearest part. See diagram opposite.

Note that "adjoining" is defined at (4) below to include any owner within the stated distance, so that, as shown in the diagram, there may be two adjoining buildings on the same side. The six metres is measured from the part of the construction or excavation which cuts the 45 degree plane to the nearest part of the adjoining building, whether wall or footing.

six metre notice diagram

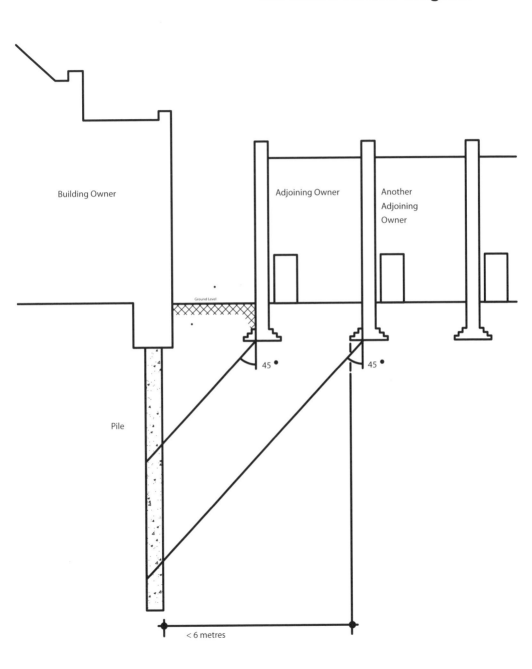

Building Owner

Adjoining Owner

Another
Adjoining
Owner

Ground Level

Pile

45 •

45 •

< 6 metres

COMMENT
The purpose of this section is to notify an adjoining owner of the intention to excavate within 3 and 6 metres of an adjoining owner's building or structure. It does not confer a right to gain access over an adjoining owner's land to erect a building as mentioned in s.6(1) and (2).

As to whether a building owner has a right of access onto an adjoining owner's land under section 8 to excavate his (the building owner's) land or construct foundations, the Working Party's view is that work under section 6 is work "in pursuance of this Act" (section 8) and that the building owner is entitled to have access under section 8.

However, the members of the Working Party have different reasons for reaching this view. Three members of the Working Party believe that any works for which notice is served is work "in pursuance of this Act". Two members of the Working Party believe that work "in pursuance of this Act" is restricted to work requiring the consent of the owners or is the subject of an award.

(3) The building owner may, and if required by the adjoining owner shall, at his own expense underpin or otherwise strengthen or safeguard the foundations of the building or structure of the adjoining owner so far as may be necessary.

INTERPRETATION

The building owner may decide that the adjoining building will need some kind of safeguarding or, alternatively, the adjoining owner may ask for it. If they do not agree, dispute resolution under s.10 ensues.

COMMENT

Note the words: "at his own expense", which is different from where other works are required by the adjoining owner.

The degree of safeguarding, and therefore the costs to be met by the building owner, will be commensurate with the risk posed by the proposed works to the adjoining owner's property. Very often no underpinning or other strengthening may be needed.

The building owner does not have any express right to underpin an adjoining owner's property under section 6 although he does have a right to underpin a party structure and party fence wall under s.2(2)(a) for which a separate notice should be served.

s.6(4)

(4) Where the buildings or structures of different owners are within the respective distances mention in subsections (1) and (2) the owners of those buildings or structures shall be deemed to be adjoining owners for the purposes of this section.

INTERPRETATION
The specified distances are the definitive control, so that the intervention of, for example, a narrow strip of land belonging to a third party, does not disentitle to notice or protection a neighbour whose land does not immediately adjoin, but whose building may be affected. This is particularly relevant when a footpath or narrow street, in council or other ownership, separates a site, on which excavation is intended, from the nearest building. It also applies, however, if a second building, beyond the immediately adjacent building, is within the specified distance – more commonly in the case of the six-metre than in that of the three-metre provisions.

COMMENT
Where a freeholder retains the whole, or part of, the external wall, a leaseholder is nevertheless an adjoining owner under s.6 provided his demise falls within 3 or 6 metres of the excavation.

In a multi-storey and multi-tenanted building, it is advisable to serve notice on every adjoining owner within the 3 or 6 metres measured horizontally irrespective of how high up the building their demise is.

(5) In any case where this section applies the building owner shall, at least one month before beginning to excavate, or excavate for and erect a building or structure, serve on the adjoining owner a notice indicating his proposals and stating whether he proposes to underpin or otherwise strengthen or safeguard the foundations of the building or structure of the adjoining owner.

INTERPRETATION

A building owner must give at least one month's notice of what works he intends, including whether he proposes to do anything about the adjoining owner's foundations by way of safeguarding or strengthening. Often he may intend to do no such works to adjoining foundations, and there may be no necessity to do works to them, but he must say in the notice if he is doing them, in order that the adjoining owner may have the opportunity to disagree and request some foundation works if he considers these necessary. Disputes as to necessity are settled in accordance with s.10. A notice which does not provide the specified information is invalid.

COMMENT

As with the comment under s.3(1), notifiable work commencing without notice is illegal and will remain so until regularised between the owners who may elect to appoint surveyors to settle the matter in accordance with s.10 of the Act.

s.6.(6)(a)&(b)

(6) The notice referred to in subsection (5) shall be accompanied by plans and sections showing –

(a) the site and depth of any excavation the building owner proposes to make;

(b) if he proposes to erect a building or structure, its site.

INTERPRETATION
A notice under this section must be accompanied by plans, and show the site and depth of any proposed excavation and the site of any building which it is proposed to erect. There may be no building, since the excavation could be for a drain. The information as to depth is essential, in order to allow the adjoining owner to take an informed view about the need for underpinning or other protection.

COMMENT
Whilst not an obligation upon the building owner, it is helpful to show the location of the adjoining owner's building on the plan in relation to the building owner's site.

In respect of piles, the Working Party consider that stating the depth on a drawing constitutes "showing".

(7) If an owner on whom a notice referred to in subsection (5) has been served does not serve a notice indicating his consent to it within the period of fourteen days beginning with the day on which the notice referred to in subsection (5) was served, he shall be deemed to have dissented from the notice and a dispute shall be deemed to have arisen between the parties.

INTERPRETATION
If consent is not given within fourteen days, a dispute is deemed to have arisen. The provisions of s.10 will then apply.

COMMENT
The notice of consent must be in writing but a deemed dissent could be changed to consent later if the parties so wished but would still be subject to a formal determination by way of an award by the surveyors if they are appointed.

s.6(8)(a)&(b)

(8) The notice referred to in subsection (5) shall cease to have effect if the work to which the notice relates –

    (a) has not begun within the period of twelve months beginning with the day on which the notice was served; and

    (b) is not prosecuted with due diligence.

INTERPRETATION

A notice and the entitlement to do works expire after twelve months or if the work is not carried out with reasonable speed. If work does not begin for 12 months after notice and an award has not been made, the notice ceases to have effect and a new notice must be served.

COMMENT

This provides some safeguard against the works being allowed to drag on unnecessarily, and certainly prevents a building owner from serving notice just in case he ever wants to do the work, and then leaving it inactive for several years, thus creating lasting uncertainty for the adjoining owner.

If the work starts and then stops for an unreasonable length of time, a new notice must be served unless the works are being carried out under an award in which case the terms of the award will apply.

(9) On completion of any work executed in pursuance of this section the building owner shall if so requested by the adjoining owner supply him with particulars including plans and sections of the work.

INTERPRETATION
The adjoining owner is entitled to "as-built" drawings, plans and sections, if he requests them, on completion of the work.

COMMENT
If minor variations have been agreed in the course of the works by the owners or by the surveyors, under s.7(5), then the adjoining owner may wish to have a definitive set of plans.

Note that the provision to request "as-built" drawings only relates to works under s.6

(10) Nothing in this section shall relieve the building owner from any liability to which he would otherwise be subject for injury to any adjoining owner or any adjoining occupier by reason of work executed by him.

INTERPRETATION

Although an adjoining owner may have consented to the works, or his surveyor has concurred in the preparation of an award, this does not mean that the building owner is exonerated from liability if any damage results from his activities. He is still responsible for the consequences of his action.

Rights etc

7. – (1) A building owner shall not exercise any right conferred on him by this Act in such a manner or at such time as to cause unnecessary inconvenience to any adjoining owner or any adjoining occupier.

INTERPRETATION

Building works by their nature are necessarily inconvenient. Any work to a party wall is likely to have potential for causing inconvenience to the adjoining owner or occupiers, and this simply has to be expected. What amounts to "necessary" inconvenience must be a question of fact in every case. However, the building owner must be reasonable, and if he causes inconvenience which could have been avoided by doing the works in some other reasonable way, he will be in breach of this section. The surveyors may have to decide whether an alternative method of working will avoid unnecessary inconvenience. There is no right to cause unnecessary inconvenience in return for compensation.

Hours of working may be limited, under this section, by award, using s.10(12). A fair allowance is to be paid (see s.11(6)) in respect of inconvenience caused by works carried out under s.2(2)(e), irrespective of whether that inconvenience was necessary or unnecessary. In respect of all other works, damage for nuisance or breach of statutory duty could be claimed if unnecessary inconvenience was caused but cannot be awarded by the surveyors.

s.7.(1)(continued)

COMMENT
Note that the provisions of environmental health, noise and other related legislation will all apply, and must be complied with by the building owner.

It does not matter whether it is more expensive or inconvenient for the building owner to undertake the work in a way that is less inconvenient to the adjoining owner.

(2)   The building owner shall compensate any adjoining owner and any adjoining occupier for any loss or damage which may result to any of them by reason of any work executed in pursuance of this Act.

INTERPRETATION

A building owner must compensate the adjoining owner and occupiers for any loss or damage caused by the notifiable work. This means direct loss, related to works carried out under the Act, and does not include, for example, claims for loss of trade caused by the presence of a building site next door. If, however, the work under the Act itself was of such a nature as to cause, for example, a restaurant to close, that would be covered.

Refer to s.11(8) for payments in lieu of making good damage.

COMMENT

It is for the appointed surveyors to determine what compensation, if any, is to be paid. In respect of damage or compensation which is in dispute, it is the surveyors' duty to agree upon the extent of damage, the making good required and in the event of a financial payment, the amount to be given to the adjoining owner.

(3) Where a building owner in exercising any right conferred on him by this Act lays open any part of the adjoining land or building he shall at his own expense make and maintain so long as may be necessary a proper hoarding, shoring or fans or temporary construction for the protection of the adjoining land or building and the security of any adjoining occupier.

INTERPRETATION

Where parts of the adjoining property's structure are opened up or left exposed as part of the work – referred to as being "laid open" – (for example when a party wall is taken down and rebuilt) the building owner must provide temporary walls or hoardings for the protection of the adjoining property.

COMMENT

This can be a very elaborate and costly business, which is why a party wall is often older than the buildings on either side of it, having been left intact when redevelopment has taken place on both sides.

The right to lay open should not be invoked without the most careful consideration of the consequences, as well as the benefits. See also s.2(2)(n).

Security to the adjoining owner's land and property must be maintained throughout the period the land and property is laid open.

As laying open only occurs in exercising a right conferred by this Act it will only arise if a party wall or party fence wall is demolished, not a boundary wall or fence on the land of the building owner.

(4) Nothing in this Act shall authorise the building owner to place special foundations on land of an adjoining owner without his previous consent in writing.

INTERPRETATION
Special foundations, as defined in s.20, (which includes reinforced concrete construction) can only be placed on the adjoining owner's land with his written permission. This provision is absolute; the adjoining owner cannot be forced to accept such works. If he does accepts them – in writing – then other provisions as to consequential costs come into play under s.11(10).

COMMENT
It is important to read the definition of special foundations under s.20 and the comment thereon.

s.7(5)(a)&(b)

(5) Any works executed in pursuance of this Act shall-

    (a) comply with the provisions of statutory requirements; and

    (b) be executed in accordance with such plans, sections and particulars as may be agreed between the owners or in the event of dispute determined in accordance with section 10;

and no deviation shall be made from those plans, sections and particulars except such as may be agreed between the owners (or surveyors acting on their behalf) or in the event of dispute determined in accordance with section 10.

INTERPRETATION
This is an extremely important section as it states that there must be a consent between owners or an award before the works can be executed.

Any works carried out under the Act must conform to other statutory requirements, and must not deviate from those agreed or settled under the dispute provisions of s.10. Owners or surveyors may agree variations to the works for which notice was originally given.

COMMENT
This obviates the need for new notices for minor variations of the sort which frequently arise in the course of construction works. For example, additional cutting becomes necessary as the work proceeds, or a revised detail of a parapet is produced. It would be wise to record any such agreed variations in writing, or by award.

It has been suggested that a building owner might lawfully proceed with notifiable work after the expiration of the relevant notice period, whether or not there is a consent from the adjoining owner or an award made. This is not a view shared by the majority and this section clearly states that the works can only commence once agreement is reached or an award entered into.

Rights of entry
s.8.(1)

8.- (1)   A building owner, his servants, agents and workmen may during usual working hours enter and remain on any land or premises for the purpose of executing any work in pursuance of this Act and may remove any furniture or fittings or take any other action necessary for that purpose.

INTERPRETATION
Subsection (1) gives a right to the building owner and his representatives to enter on adjoining land and remain there in order to carry out work in pursuance of the Act, but the crucial work is "necessary". It is not a licence to use next door's premises for the convenience of the building owner, stacking materials on next door's roof , for example, when they could perfectly easily – if perhaps not quite so conveniently – be stored on the building owner's side.

This subsection allows the building owner to erect scaffolding (when necessary) on the adjoining owner's land for as long as it is needed. "Usual working hours", for scaffolding, are 24 hours a day.

COMMENT
The provisions of this section cannot be used to obtain access to property whose owner does not respond to notice. The proper procedure is to serve notice under s.8(3) and (4) and where appropriate appoint a surveyor under s.10(4) and, if necessary, make an award under s.10(7).

An appointed surveyor's rights are separately dealt with at subsection 5. It is rarely necessary to remove furniture or fittings and the surveyors will need to consider if this would cause "unnecessary inconvenience" in any event.

See also comment under s,1 for access.

s.8(2)

(2) If the premises are closed, the building owner, his agents and workmen may, if accompanied by a constable or other police officer, break open any fences or doors in order to enter the premises.

INTERPRETATION
If the premises are closed, a policeman can be asked to accompany those with a right of entry and the door or fence may be broken open.

Closed is regarded to mean secured shut thereby requiring to be "broken into".

COMMENT
This right is very rarely needed, and should only be exercised in the case of absolute necessity, and as a last resort. All actions taken should be carefully recorded.

(3) No land or premises may be entered by any person under subsection (1) unless the building owner serves on the owner and the occupier of the land or premises –

    (a) in case of emergency, such notice of the intention to enter as may be reasonably practicable;

    (b) in any other case, such notice of the intention to enter as complies with subsection (4).

INTERPRETATION
As much notice as is reasonably practicable must be given in cases of emergency and, in every other case, at least fourteen day's notice.

Note that a notice must be served on the owner and the occupier.

COMMENT
An emergency might arise if damage were caused to a party structure during demolition or reconstruction of the building owner's premises, and that damage needed instant and urgent repair.

For service of notice, see subsection (4) and s.15.

For notice served on an occupier who is not an "owner" under the Act, a description of the intended works and the procedures which have been followed should be given.

s.8(4)

(4) Notice complies with this subsection if it is served in a period of not less than fourteen days ending with the day of the proposed entry.

INTERPRETATION
If the need for entry is routine, a full two weeks' notice in writing must be given.

(5) A surveyor appointed or selected under section 10 may during usual working hours enter and remain on any land or premises for the purpose of carrying out the object for which he is appointed or selected.

INTERPRETATION

Most awards (see s.10(12)) specify the freedom of access to be allowed to the appointed surveyors. This subsection gives a general right to surveyors to go on to either side of the wall (or boundary) for the purposes of the Act. A third surveyor, therefore, who may be unknown to both building and adjoining owner, has a right of entry if he needs it to settle any disagreement between the first two named surveyors or the owners.

COMMENT

If the surveyors consider it necessary to take a schedule of condition of the adjoining property before works commence and access has not been made available, they can call upon the provisions of this section to gain entry.

s.8(6)(a)&(b)

(6) No land or premises may be entered by a surveyor under subsection (5) unless the building owner who is a party to the dispute concerned serves on the owner and the occupier of the land or premises –

(a) in case of emergency, such notice of the intention to enter as may be reasonably practicable;

(b) in any other case, such notice of the intention to enter as complies with subsection (4).

INTERPRETATION
Note that notice must be served on the owner _and_ the occupier.

As this subsection derives directly from section 8(5) which gives a right of entry for the surveyors to enter either the building owner's or adjoining owner's land, the Working Party believe the "building owner" should mean the owner who requires the surveyors to have access. The intention must mean "the owner of the building" must give notice. However, this is not what the Act states.

If an adjoining owner refuses access then notice can be given by a building owner under s.8(6) but not the other way around because s.8(6) refers to a building owner giving notice. If the building owner refuses entry for the surveyors, then the surveyors can make an award determining that access must be provided and refer to s.16(1). Alternatively the adjoining owner may need to demonstrate to a court that the building owner is obstructing access.

9. - Nothing in this Act shall –

    (a) authorise any interference with an easement of light or other easements in or relating to a party wall; or

    (b) prejudicially affect any right of any person to preserve or restore any right or other thing in or connected with a party wall in case of the party wall being pulled down or rebuilt.

INTERPRETATION

Paragraph (a) of this section makes it clear that the Act does not authorise interference with an existing easement especially one of light. The fact that the building owner may have a right under this Act to raise the party wall does not, therefore, entitle him to affect the adjoining owner's right of light. Paragraph (b) expressly allows the retention of an existing easement, even if the wall is pulled down and rebuilt. Although, therefore, there is no right to form a window in a party wall, if one already exists the building owner has the right, so far as this Act is concerned, to reproduce it if he pulls down and then rebuilds a party wall.

Other easements such as the right to retain overhanging eaves or subterranean foundations, are specifically overridden in s.2, and this clause does not negate those exceptions.

COMMENT
It is quite wrong to refuse to sign an award "because rights of light may be affected". The inclusion in the award of a clause to make clear that any such easement is unaffected, for lay benefit, can be helpful.

10.-(1) Where a dispute arises or is deemed to have arisen between a building owner and an adjoining owner in respect of any matter connected with any work to which this Act relates either –

    (a)   both parties shall concur in the appointment of one surveyor (in this section referred to as an "agreed surveyor"); or

    (b)   each party shall appoint a surveyor and the two surveyors so appointed shall forthwith select a third surveyor (all of whom are in this section referred to as "the three surveyors").

INTERPRETATION
Subsection (1) provides that where a dispute arises or is deemed to have arisen, if possible both parties should agree on the appointment of a single surveyor to resolve any differences. Alternatively, each side appoints a surveyor, and the two surveyors select a third, to act as umpire if they are unable to agree. All surveyors appointed under this section are expected to act impartially: they are not agents for those who appoint them. The term "appointing owner" is therefore used, rather than "client" to describe the party who appoints the surveyor.

COMMENT
It is highly desirable that the agreed surveyor solution should be adopted whenever possible. There is often no matter upon which experienced surveyors will disagree, and therefore no need for each side to appoint separately. Costs will be minimised if only one surveyor is involved.

When two surveyors are needed, and/or appointed, they should immediately make their selection of the third surveyor, before any other matter can become contentious. He does not need to be contacted to give his consent to be named, but if disagreements are in prospect it can be helpful to find out if he is likely to be available.

When one party alleges that a wall is a party wall, and the other that it is not, the proper thing to do for the owner who says that it is one, is to use all the powers of the Act to proceed to serve notice, appointing surveyors, etc. The owner who denies can appeal an award made by the surveyors which states it is a party wall. The surveyors can determine whether the building owner has the right to execute the work for which he has served notice.

Any written consent given by an adjoining owner for the notifiable work to be done does not obviate the possibility at a dispute might still arise out of the work during its progress or after it has been done. In which case, surveyors will have to be appointed to determine the matter.

(2) All appointments and selections made under this section shall be in writing and shall not be rescinded by either party.

INTERPRETATION
Note that all appointments must be in writing and that they cannot be changed or withdrawn at will. A surveyor may only be replaced if the requirements of subsection (5) are fulfilled, and those are brought about by the surveyor himself. An appointing owner cannot chop and change because he does not like what his surveyor does, or because he wants to frustrate the procedures of the Act.

All appointments and selections are personal and can only change in accordance with subsections (3), (5) and (9).

COMMENT
A surveyor appointed by an adjoining owner should immediately inform the building owner or the surveyor appointed by the building owner of his appointment to avoid the possibility of an appointment of a different surveyor under section 10(4).

As good practice, an appointed surveyor should ask for a copy of the other surveyor's letter of appointment to act in accordance with s.10 at the outset of discussions.

Owners find it hard to understand that the surveyor they have appointed is not there to do their bidding but to administer the Act impartially.

Appointed surveyors should take the time where necessary to explain to appointing owners that their position is not that of an agent promoting any cause, but that they are fulfilling a statutory duty and they are there to administer the Act impartially and fairly.

(3) If an agreed surveyor –

  (a) refuses to act;

  (b) neglects to act for a period of ten days beginning with the day on which either party serves a request on him:

  (c) dies before the dispute is settled; or

  (d) becomes or deems himself incapable of acting,

  the proceedings for settling such dispute shall begin *de novo*.

INTERPRETATION

Subsection (3) deals with the situation if an agreed (single) surveyor refuses or neglects for ten days to act, dies or becomes unable to proceed. In that case the selection procedure begins afresh. He may become incapable by illness or disability, or because he is emigrating, and he may deem himself incapable because of personal or professional circumstances or because a conflict of interest arises.

COMMENT

Note that a timetable begins to operate in this subsection, and correct use of the procedures and time constraints ensures that matters are not unreasonably delayed.

(4) If either party to the dispute –

    (a) refuses to appoint a surveyor under subsection (1)(b), or

    (b) neglects to appoint a surveyor under subsection (1)(b) for a period of ten days beginning with the day on which the other party serves a request on him,

the other party may make the appointment on his behalf.

INTERPRETATION
The procedures of the Act cannot be frustrated by one party refusing or failing to appoint a surveyor. In that case, the other party may make the appointment, using as much care as if he were doing it for himself.

COMMENT
In a large development, when many party walls are involved, a building owner will often appoint as adjoining owner's surveyor, a surveyor already involved on the site, appointed by another adjoining owner.

In his selection of a surveyor for another party, the building owner should avoid any suggestion that he is choosing someone who will be subservient to his wishes, and the surveyor so appointed must equally be seen to have proper regard for those on whose behalf he is appointed, not just for those who appointed him.

The surveyor can make this appointment on behalf of the building owner if he has due authority from the building owner to do so.

(5) If, before the dispute is settled, a surveyor appointed under paragraph (b) of subsection (1) by a party to the dispute dies, or becomes or deems himself incapable of acting, the party who appointed him may appoint another surveyor in his place with the same power and authority.

INTERPRETATION

The party who appointed a surveyor in the first place may replace him if he dies or becomes incapable of acting. He does not have the power to replace a willing and active surveyor.

COMMENT

The use of the word "may" is curious, because if the dispute has not been settled, ie determined by an award, a surveyor must be appointed to enable the statutory process to be completed. Note that if a third surveyor has been selected, an award can be made by the third surveyor and the remaining surveyor.

This proviso "may appoint" might well apply if the situation occurred after an award is made, but the Working Party recommends a new surveyor should always be appointed as "disputes" may arise during the course of the works or in relation to damage.

The Working Party considers "incapable" to mean a physical or mental inability to fulfil the statutory role for which the surveyor has accepted the appointment or if circumstances change which take the surveyor out of the definition of a "surveyor" in s.20.

Incapability must not be used as a cloak to hide behind a refusal to act.

(6) If a surveyor -

    (a) appointed under paragraph (b) of subsection (1) by a party to the dispute; or

    (b) appointed under subsection (4) or (5),

refuses to act effectively, the surveyor of the other party may proceed to act *ex parte* and anything so done by him shall be as effectual as if he has been an agreed surveyor.

(7) If a surveyor –

    (a) appointed under paragraph (b) of subsection (1) by a party to the dispute; or

    (b) appointed under subsection (4) or (5),

neglects to act effectively for a period of ten days beginning with the day on which either party or the surveyor of the other party serves a request on him, the surveyor of the other party may proceed to act *ex parte* in respect of the subject matter of the request and anything so done by him shall be as effectual as if he had been an agreed surveyor.

INTERPRETATION
If an appointed surveyor refuses to act effectively, the surveyor appointed by the other party may immediately proceed to act *ex parte*. If he fails to respond to a request to act, then ten days must elapse before the right to act *ex parte* comes into effect.

s.10(6)(a)&(b) and (7)(a)&(b)*(continued)*

Thereafter, the other surveyor must act completely impartially, even more so, if possible, than he was already doing, and make an award (or act in other ways) as if he were the agreed surveyor. In the case of failure to act, rather than refusal, the right to proceed *ex parte* only extends to the matters in respect of which the other surveyor has been asked to act and failed.

COMMENT
There can be some argument about what acting "effectively" is. Merely to acknowledge a draft award, or to reply that one did not like it, would not qualify; nor would a succession of petty quibbles. A reasoned response would certainly be "effective".

An attempt to act precipitately and unreasonably ex parte, would risk the award being set aside by the court and the costs visited upon the party who appointed the surveyor who acted in this way.

Note that s.10(6) relates to "refusal" and s.10(7) to "neglect". If you serve under s.10(6) and the other surveyor "neglects" to act you cannot proceed ex parte. To avoid being caught between the two serve notice requiring a surveyor to act under both subsections.

(8) If either surveyor appointed under subsection (1)(b) by a party to the dispute refuses to select a third surveyor under subsection (1) or (9), or neglects to do so for a period of ten days beginning with the day on which the other surveyor serves a request on him –

(a) the appointing officer; or

(b) in cases where the relevant appointing officer or his employer is a party to the dispute, the Secretary of State,

may on the application of either surveyor select a third surveyor who shall have the same power and authority as if he had been selected under subsection (1) or subsection (9).

INTERPRETATION
This subsection provides for the selection of a third surveyor by the local authority or, where the local authority are party to the proceedings, by the Secretary of State, in cases where either surveyor fails to agree upon such a selection. The appointing officer is defined in s.20 and it is up to the local authority to nominate someone – the principal building control officer, perhaps – to exercise those powers.

COMMENT
A local authority is the authority which administers Building Regulations for the area where the work is to be carried out.

A person appointed to select the third surveyor could levy an administration charge so the appointed surveyor should keep the owner properly informed of the process adopted and the reasons why.

s.10(9)(a)(b)&(c)

(9) If a third surveyor selected under subsection (1)(b) -

(a) refuses to act;

(b) neglects to act for a period of ten days beginning with the day on which either party or the surveyor appointed by either party serves a request on him; or

(c) dies, or becomes or deems himself incapable of acting, before the dispute is settled,

the other two of the three surveyors shall forthwith select another surveyor in his place with the same power and authority.

INTERPRETATION
If the selected third surveyor cannot or will not act as set out in the subsection, the other two surveyors must immediately select another: if there are problems, subsection (8) should be followed.

COMMENT
If an award is made by the first two surveyors, they may include a clause which provides for the replacement third surveyor to be selected by the appointing officer at the local authority if they cannot agree upon a substitute. It is not correct for the award to state that the replacement third surveyor is to be chosen by the president of one of the professional bodies.

(10) The agreed surveyor or as the case may be the three surveyors or any two of them shall settle by award any matter –

(a) which is connected with any work to which this Act relates, and

(b) which is in dispute between the building owner and the adjoining owner.

INTERPRETATION

The surveyors are empowered to settle by award any matter arising out of the Act in dispute between the two owners. It is possible that the work could have started before notice was served, but that work cannot be covered by a subsequent notice and the surveyors have no power to settle any dispute arising in connection therewith unless the parties subscribe to the process or a court directs them to do so.

If there is an agreed surveyor, he still has a duty to publish an award to both parties so that each knows the rights and responsibilities of the other – and the right of appeal under subsection (17).

COMMENT

If two surveyors make an award, it is rare that the third surveyor is one of them, unless one surveyor is clearly in the wrong in a disagreement. In that case the third surveyor may join the other in signing.

s.10(10)(a)&(b)(continued)

Surveyors should be careful not to deal with matters outside the Act, and hence outside their powers. The position of the boundary between ownerships does not lie in their determination under the Act, but they can determine whether a building owner has the right to carry out works for which he has served notice.

(11) Either of the parties or either of the surveyors appointed by the parties may call upon the third surveyor selected in pursuance of this section to determine the disputed matters and he shall make the necessary award.

INTERPRETATION
Subsection (11) empowers either surveyor or either party to call in the third surveyor to make an award.

COMMENT
It will usually be a surveyor who does this, but he should first advise his appointing owner about the costs and delays which might result. A building owner especially might be prepared to concede an unreasonable demand rather than be held up while the third surveyor makes his determination.

In the case where relations between an owner and an appointed surveyor become bad, for whatever reason, the owner can call upon the third surveyor directly to make an award.

s.10(12)(a)(b)&(c)

(12) An award may determine –

    (a) the right to execute any work;

    (b) the time and manner of executing any work; and

    (c) any other matter arising out of or incidental to the dispute including the costs of making the award;

but any period appointed by the award for executing any work shall not unless otherwise agreed between the building owner and the adjoining owner begin to run until after the expiration of the period prescribed by this Act for service of the notice in respect of which the dispute arises or is deemed to have arisen.

INTERPREATION

This is a wide jurisdiction but it means that any questions connected with a dispute arising out of, or incidental to, the Act, or out of any works carried out pursuant to notices may be settled simply and cheaply by the procedures of this section. If, for example, damage occurs to an adjoining owner's premises, the surveyors can decide whether it was caused by the building owner's works, and if so can agree the cost or manner of rectifying it.

COMMENT

There is no duty imposed upon a building owner's surveyor (or the building owner) to tell the other side that works are complete. When the building side thinks that they are, it is certainly a good idea to tell the neighbours.

If the adjoining owner's surveyor wants to put a time limit on the work, it should be done in the award, and, if the building owner's surveyor disagrees the third surveyor can be asked to rule.

All decisions taken by the surveyors, or matters agreed by them, constitute a statutory determination and must be subject to appeal by the owners if they disagree. These decisions must be the subject of an award and published to the owners.

The owners must be notified of their rights to challenge the decision under s.10(17).

s.10(13)(a)(b)&(c)

(13) The reasonable costs incurred in –

    (a) making or obtaining an award under this section;

    (b) reasonable inspections of work to which the award relates; and

    (c) any other matter arising out of the dispute,

shall be paid by such of the parties as the surveyor or surveyors making the award determine.

INTERPRETATION

The Act does not say, contrary to what many seem to think, that the building owner shall pay the fees. Usually he does, but it is for the surveyors to award so.

COMMENT

A case where fees might be borne equally is where both sides are carrying out works simultaneously. Instead of trying to separate out fees due in respect of building and adjoining owners' work on each side, they might agree to each bear their own.

If an engineer, or any specialist adviser, is needed by the surveyors his fees should be included with those of the surveyor, but it is as well for surveyors to agree beforehand that engineering advice is reasonably required. The advice that is needed from an engineer by an adjoining owner's surveyor is not a line-by-line check of all the building owner's engineer's calculations, but an overview, (supported perhaps by a random check or two) of the latter's work, to ensure that it is being properly done.

Remember, as set out elsewhere, that the building owner remains responsible for the results of his actions, and he is not let off the hook if the adjoining owner's team check everything or nothing.

Solicitors' fees need rarely to be included, but if they have been incurred in "obtaining" an award, because the other side have needed legal pressure to make them comply with the Act, then that is an exception. Advice merely on the implications of notice or the Act does not so qualify.

Claims for excessive fees can only be challenged by going to the third surveyor. The third surveyor should issue directions on the payment of his fees in his award.

(14) Where the surveyors appointed by the parties make an award the surveyors shall serve it forthwith on the parties.

INTERPRETATION

An award must be promptly sent by the surveyors to the owners. It really should be forwarded to the owner on the day that the signed copy comes into the hands of his appointed surveyor.

COMMENT

It is good practice for each surveyor to confirm to the other that they award has been served upon their respective owners.

(15) Where an award is made by the third surveyor –

    (a) he shall, after payment of the costs of the award, serve it forthwith on the parties or their appointed surveyors; and

    (b) if it is served on their appointed surveyors, they shall serve it forthwith on the parties.

INTERPRETATION

The third surveyor must deliver his award as soon as his fee has been paid and, if sent to the surveyors, the latter must promptly send it on to the owners.

COMMENT

It is usual for the third surveyor to announce that his award may be taken up on payment of his (stated) fees, and immediately he receives them, either party from each side or wholly from the party more anxious to obtain the award, he signs and sends out two copies of the award, usually to the surveyors.

His award will confirm which party is responsible for the costs of his award.

(16) The award shall be conclusive and shall not except as provided by this section be questioned in any court.

INTERPRETATION
An award is final, unless properly challenged in the courts. After fourteen days, therefore, as laid down in subsection (17), the award is absolute and cannot be appealed, unless it is bad in itself. A decision that a building owner's works had caused damage could not be appealed after time had run; a purported award by a surveyor who had not been properly appointed could be.

COMMENT
However, a building owner remains liable for the results of his actions. He would not be immune from the consequences of subsequent subsidence, for example, merely because no award had been made in that respect earlier, or even because an award had been made exonerating him from having caused some other damage.

(17) Either of the parties to the dispute may, within the period of fourteen days beginning with the day on which an award made under this section is served on him, appeal to the county court against the award and the county court may–

(a) rescind the award or modify it in such manner as the court thinks fit; and

(b) make such order as to costs as the court thinks fit.

INTERPRETATION

Any appeal against an award must be made within fourteen days to the county court, which may rescind, modify, or uphold the award, and make any order as to costs.

COMMENT

Strictly speaking, there is no respondent to such an appeal, but the owner other than the one who appeals will usually wish to be heard, and is likely to be treated by the court as a respondent. A third surveyor is definitely not party to the action if his award is appealed.

It is good practice to advise an owner of his right of appeal within fourteen days when serving the award upon him.

Note: The parties may apply to the court at any time to have the provisions of an award enforced as may be necessary.

s.11(1)&(2)

Expenses

11. -(1) Except as provided under this section expenses of work under this Act shall be defrayed by the building owner.

(2) Any dispute as to responsibility for expenses shall be settled as provided in section 10.

INTERPRETATION
Unless the Act states otherwise, the building owner will be liable for costs of work carried out under the Act.

Subsection (2) refers disputes as to costs to the surveyors to settle under the provisions of section 10.

COMMENT
Section 11(1) relates to expenses of work and not expenses of fees and costs which are dealt with under s.10(13).

(3) An expense mentioned in section 1(3)(b) shall be defrayed as there mentioned.

INTERPRETATION
Section 1(3)(b) says that when an adjoining owner agrees to the construction of a party wall or party fence wall, the owners share the cost according to the use made. That is likely to be equally in the case of a party fence wall, but may well be unequal if the building owner is going to use the wall to enclose a substantial structure.

(4) Where work is carried out in exercise of the right mentioned in section 2(2)(a), and the work is necessary on account of defect or want of repair of the structure or wall concerned, the expenses shall be defrayed by the building owner and the adjoining owner in such proportion as has regard to –

(a) the use which the owners respectively make or may make of the structure or wall concerned; and

(b) responsibility for the defect or want of repair concerned, if more than one owner makes use of the structure or wall concerned.

INTERPRETATION

Section 2(2)(a) deals with underpinning, thickening or raising a party structure, or the building owner's wall against such a structure. Only underpinning or, occasionally, thickening, is likely to be necessary because of "defect or want of repair", but in that case the costs are to be paid according to the use made of the structure or responsibility for the defect. These may sometimes conflict and have to be resolved.

Where work being carried out under s.2(2)(a) is not because of "defect or want of repair", s.11(1) prevails and the building owner pays.

(5) Where work is carried out in exercise of the right mentioned in section 2(2)(b) the expenses shall be defrayed by the building owner and the adjoining owner in such proportion as has regard to –

(a) the use which the owners respectively make or may make of the structure or wall concerned; and

(b) responsibility for the defect or want of repair concerned, if more than one owner makes use of the structure or wall concerned.

INTERPRETATION
Where defects or lack of repair are involved, costs will be apportioned according to the use of the wall and responsibility for the defect or lack of repair. As explained in relation to subsection (4), the proportions under (a) and (b) may be very different, and will need reconciliation. One owner may have neglected the wall, while the other uses it more intensively. The surveyors must apportion the costs to take proper account of both aspects.

COMMENT
An example of responsibility for a defect might be where one owner's tree has caused a party fence wall to significantly lean and become unstable. Both owners make equal use of the party fence wall but the owner of the tree will be responsible for the cost of the repair works.

(6) Where the adjoining premises are laid open in exercise of the right mentioned in section 2(2)(e) a fair allowance in respect of disturbance and inconvenience shall be paid by the building owner to the adjoining owner or occupier.

INTERPRETATION

Subsection (6) provides for payment of a suitable sum for disturbance and inconvenience when premises are laid open by the demolition of a party wall due to it being of insufficient strength or height for the building owner, since this will also inevitably involve the provision of a temporary wall, and temporary loss of space.

COMMENT

Not only may the adjoining owner be working or living in constricted space, but circulation may be disrupted, and there are likely to be at least two lots of extra cleaning to be done: when the temporary partitioning goes in, and when it comes out. As mentioned under s.7(3) the complications and cost of such an exercise means that it is usually avoided if at all possible.

This fair allowance is designed to be agreed and made before the event, compared to compensation which is assessed after the event to redress a loss caused by the work.

(7) Where a building owner proposes to reduce the height of a party wall or party fence wall under section 2(2)(m) the adjoining owner may serve a counter notice under section 4 requiring the building owner to maintain the existing height of the wall, and in such case the adjoining owner shall pay to the building owner a due proportion of the cost of the wall so far as it exceeds –

(a) two metres in height; or

(b) the height currently enclosed upon by the building of the adjoining owner.

INTERPRETATION

If an adjoining owner wants a party wall maintained to a height greater than he would normally be entitled to, he must pay a proportion of the cost of constructing that additional height. For example, it may be that the adjoining owner only uses the wall to bound his garden, but the building owner, who currently has a four-storey building, wishes to reduce the wall to garden wall height. If the adjoining owner then required the building owner to maintain the wall to a greater height than the two metres specified in s.2(2)(m), he must pay the building owner a proper proportion of the cost of the increased height which he requests.

When the adjoining owner has a building enclosed by the party wall, as well as the actual height enclosure he is entitled to a parapet by s.2(7) and does not have to pay for it. Anything more than the parapet necessary to satisfy statutory requirements or good building practice would be the subject of a payment under this subsection.

(8) Where the building owner is required to make good damage under this Act the adjoining owner has a right to require that the expenses of such making good be determined in accordance with section 10 and paid to him in lieu of the carrying out of work to make the damage good.

INTERPRETATION

The primary responsibility of a building owner is to compensate the adjoining owner or occupier for any loss or damage caused. However, where he is obliged under the Act to make good damage an adjoining owner can ask for a money payment in lieu. Although under a number of provisions in this Act the building owner is required to make good any damage, very often it will be inconvenient for the adjoining owner to have that making good done when it suits the building owner, and he will quite probably not welcome the presence of the contractor who caused the damage in the first place. In that case he may prefer to take an agreed payment for the cost of the works instead.

COMMENT

The cost of the adjoining owner's estimate may well exceed that of the building owner's on-site contractor. The resolution of such disparity would be a matter for the surveyors under s.10, but the adjoining owner's right to have money instead of works is undoubted.

The building owner's duty to make good damage only arises under s.2(3)(a), 2(4)(a), 2(5) and 2(6).

(9) Where –

    (a) works are carried out, and

    (b) some of the works are carried out at the request of the adjoining owner or in pursuance of a requirement by him,

he shall defray the expenses of carrying out the works requested or required by him.

INTERPRETATION

When the adjoining owner requests that additional work should be done, he is liable for the cost of that work. This does not include underpinning or safeguarding of his foundations, required by the adjoining owner and awarded by the surveyors, when such work is necessary because of the works undertaken for the benefit of the building owner, as laid down in s.6(3).

(10) Where –

    (a) consent in writing has been given to the construction of special foundations on land of an adjoining owner; and

    (b) the adjoining owner erects any building or structure and its cost is found to be increased by reason of the existence of the said foundations,

the owner of the building to which the said foundations belong shall, on receiving an account with any necessary invoices and other supporting documents within the period of two months beginning with the day of the completion of the work by the adjoining owner, repay to the adjoining owner so much of the cost as is due to the existence of the said foundations.

INTERPRETATION

An adjoining owner is entitled to an appropriate payment if his costs of construction are increased because of the existence of special foundations, however much later that cost may arise. The payment has to be made by the present owner of the building for which the special foundations were provided. Unless a lease provides otherwise, the owner in question will be the freeholder.

COMMENT

This may come as a considerable surprise to the latter, who may have owned the building for many years without knowing that his predecessor obtained a consent with a sting in its tail. Equally, the now building owner may be surprised to discover that he has a complicated foundation problem to deal with before he can proceed. It may be some consolation to him to learn that his increased costs are someone else's problem. In the interests of both sides' successors in title, a building owner should carefully consider the resulting complications before putting special foundations on adjoining land.

s.11(11)

(11) Where use is subsequently made by the adjoining owner of work carried out solely at the expense of the building owner the adjoining owner shall pay a due proportion of the expenses incurred by the building owner in carrying out that work; and for this purpose he shall be taken to have incurred expenses calculated by reference to what the cost of the work would be if it were carried out at the time when that subsequent use is made.

INTERPRETATION
When one party pays to raise a party wall at his own cost, and then at a later stage (and sometimes it is long after) the other party wishes also to use the raised part, the latter has to pay a proper share of the cost, based on construction costs prevailing when that later use is made.

COMMENT
In other words, if the wall cost £50 to raise in 1900, the second owner now wishes to make equal use of it, and the cost of building it today would be £5000, he has to pay £2500 for the privilege. Unless a lease or conveyance specifically states otherwise, the payment will be made to the present freeholder of the building of whose wall use is now being made, or to the successor under the same lease of the leasehold owner who carried out the work.

As a starting point when considering the amount to be paid, assume the wall to be enclosed upon or used is not there, and calculate the whole cost of building it at the time the additional use will occur. That should include standard preliminaries, access and usual design fees.

The adjoining owner entitled to the payment does not need to be the owner who built the wall.

12. – (1)   An adjoining owner may serve a notice requiring the building owner before he begins any work in the exercise of the rights conferred by this Act to give such security as may be agreed between the owners or in the event of dispute determined in accordance with section 10.

INTERPRETATION
When an adjoining owner might be exposed to having to pay for expensive reconstruction if the building owner were to leave work unfinished, the former can demand the deposit of sufficient security to cover those costs, any dispute over this to be settled in accordance with s.10.

COMMENT
This is particularly likely to be the case when a party wall is being demolished. If, for any reason, the building owner were to disappear while the wall was down, the adjoining owner would wish to have the wall re-erected as quickly as possible. It is desirable therefore that there should be money readily available to pay for that reconstruction. The subsection is not intended to make security a requisite against the ordinary possibility of damage to fabric, or the payment of fees.

The normal method of dealing with the money is to have it deposited in an account from which it can only be disbursed on the signatures of two of the three surveyors. If there is no call made on it, it is returned, together with any interest, to the building owner at the conclusion of the works.

The security should be provided before the works start. However, this issue should not prevent an award being agreed for other matters.

Commencement of work before security is in place could be prejudicial to the adjoining owner. Note that it is the adjoining owner who requests security, or by a surveyor if he has the appropriate authority. Only when the owners cannot agree upon whether security should be provided, or the amount, do the appointed surveyors deal with the issue in accordance with s.10 and make an award.

Security can only be requested if the building owner intends to exercise rights "conferred by this Act", ie he is proposing to carry out some work to the adjoining owner's land or property. If he is simply excavating his own land then the adjoining owner has no right to receive security under this section.

s.12(2)(a)&(b)

(2) Where –

(a) in the exercise of the rights conferred by this Act an adjoining owner requires the building owner to carry out any work the expenses of which are to be defrayed in whole or in part by the adjoining owner; or

(b) an adjoining owner serves a notice on the building owner under subsection (1),

the building owner may before beginning the work to which the requirement or notice relates serve a notice on the adjoining owner requiring him to give such security as may be agreed between the owners or in the event of dispute determined in accordance with section 10.

INTERPRETATION
Where an adjoining owner requires the building owner to carry out additional works, the latter can similarly require a suitable security for costs.

COMMENT
This is to avoid the situation where an adjoining owner seizes the opportunity to have works done for his benefit while the building owner's contractor is on site, and then proves to be unable or unwilling to pay for those works.

Paragraph (b) is repeated from the 1930 and 1939 London Building Acts, but seems very strange. Apparently, if an adjoining owner seeks security, a building owner may ask for a reciprocal deposit. It has been suggested this is an error and that it should refer to section 4 subsection (1) and relate to a counter notice served by the adjoining owner.

(3) If within the period of one month beginning with –

    (a) the day on which a notice is served under subsection (2); or

    (b) in the event of dispute, the date of determination by the surveyor or surveyors,

the adjoining owner does not comply with the notice or the determination, the requirement or notice by him to which the building owner's notice under that subsection relates shall cease to have effect.

INTERPRETATION

If an adjoining owner does not respond properly to a request for, or an award of, security under subsection (2), or to a determination by surveyors in the event of a dispute, his request for additional work is deemed to have lapsed. The building owner is thereafter under no obligation to carry out the work requested by the adjoining owner.

COMMENT

The periods of notice are fairly short in these subsections, since the building owner should not be required to hold up his works because of requests by an adjoining owner who is not prepared to back these requests with the security sought by the building owner.

13. – (1) Within the period of two months beginning with the day of the completion of any work executed by a building owner of which the expenses are to be wholly or partially defrayed by an adjoining owner in accordance with section 11 the building owner shall serve on the adjoining owner an account in writing showing –

(a)   particulars and expenses of the work; and

(b)   any deductions to which the adjoining owner or any other person is entitled in respect of old materials or otherwise;

and in preparing the account the work shall be estimated and valued at fair average rates and prices according to the nature of the work, the locality and cost of labour and materials prevailing at the time when the work is executed.

INTERPRETATION
When the building owner requires a contribution to the cost of works from an adjoining owner, he must provide suitable evidence, and the parties must then agree the accounts.

This subsection, (1), provides that when the adjoining owner is due to contribute towards costs, the building owner has to supply him with accounts and bills within two months after the works have been completed, and sets out the matters to be considered when preparing the account.

Local factors are to be taken into consideration, so that clearly the level of fees and costs will vary from place to place.

COMMENT
It is essential to ensure that the account is served within 2 months of completion of the relevant works. The right to recover is lost if the account is not served within this 2 month period.

(2) Within the period of one month beginning with the day of service of the said account the adjoining owner may serve on the building owner a notice stating any objection he may have thereto and thereupon a dispute shall be deemed to have arisen between the parties.

(3) If within that period of one month the adjoining owner does not serve notice under subsection (2) he shall be deemed to have no objection to the account.

INTERPRETATION
The adjoining owner has one month to object to the account presented, and the provisions of s.10 apply to any disputes which arise.

If the adjoining owner does not object within that month, he is deemed to have accepted the account and the sum is recoverable in accordance with s.17.

COMMENT
It is observed under subsection (2) that an objection to an account leads to an actual dispute and should be dealt with by the surveyors under s.10.

14. -(1) All expenses to be defrayed by an adjoining owner in accordance with an account served under section 13 shall be paid by the adjoining owner.

(2) Until an adjoining owner pays to the building owner such expenses as aforesaid the property in any works executed under this Act to which the expenses relate shall be vested solely in the building owner.

INTERPRETATION
Subsection (1) states that accounts delivered under s.13 must be duly settled by the adjoining owner, which seems self-evident.

The building owner retains the ownership of any works unless and until the adjoining owner pays his due share.

COMMENT
Ownership of works carried out for the benefit of the adjoining owner is, of course, no great comfort for the building owner.

15. - (1) A notice or other document required or authorised to be served under this Act may be served on a person–

  (a) by delivery it to him in person;

  (b) by sending it by post to him at his usual or last known residence or place of business in the United Kingdom; or

  (c) in the case of a body corporate, by delivering it to the secretary or clerk of the body corporate at its registered or principal office or sending it by post to the secretary or clerk of that body corporate at that office.

INTERPRETATION
This section lays down how service of notices is to be effected, depending upon whether the owner is an individual or a body corporate, and is self-explanatory.

COMMENT
Post is the usual method. The wording of this section does not include electronic transmission.

There are no set rules which establish when a notice will be considered to have been received. As guidance, the earliest date on which a notice should be presumed to have been served (and see also notice for section 10(4) and (7)) should be as follows:-

Method of service	Presumed day of service
First class post	Second day after it was posted
Document exchange	Second day after it was left at the document exchange
Delivering the document or leaving it at the address	The day after it was delivered or left at the address

2. In the case of a notice or other document required or authorised to be served under this Act on a person as owner of premises, it may alternatively be served by –

    (a) addressing it "the owner" of the premises (naming them), and

    (b) delivering it to a person on the premises or, if no person to whom it can be delivered is found there, fixing it to a conspicuous part of the premises.

INTERPRETATION

The name of the adjoining owner is not needed for service (since sometimes it may not be known) and if it is necessary to serve notice on him in respect of his ownership of certain premises, he may be addressed simply as "the owner", and the notice either delivered to someone in the building in question or fixed prominently to the premises.

COMMENT

The fixing is usually by a drawing pin stuck in the front door.

If serving notice to "the owner", this must not be by post but in accordance with s.15(2)(b) and this may also apply to serving a request to appoint a surveyor and serving the award if the adjoining owner is not known at the time of service.

16. - (1) If –

    (a) an occupier of land or premises refuses to permit a person to do anything which he is entitled to do with regard to the land or premises under section 8(1) or (5); and

    (b) the occupier knows or has reasonable cause to believe that the person is so entitled,

the occupier is guilty of an offence.

INTERPRETATION
It is an offence for an occupier to refuse entry to someone authorised to enter a building or land where they are entitled to do so under s.8, when the occupier should reasonably know that they are allowed to enter. The occupier may not necessarily be the "owner" but he should have received a notice under s.8(3) and 8(6).

s.16(2)(a)&(b)

(2) If –

    (a) a person hinders or obstructs a person in attempting to do anything which he is entitled to do with regard to land or premises under section 8(1) or (5); and

    (b) the first-mentioned person knows or has reasonable cause to believe that the other person is so entitled,

the first-mentioned person is guilty of an offence.

INTERPRETATION
Anyone who obstructs someone who has a right to be on premises is guilty of an offence if he knows, or should know, that the other person has a right to be there. The person obstructed could be a builder or a surveyor, for example, and the person doing the obstructing could be the tenant of the property or a site foreman. (Or it could be the other way round).

(3) A person guilty of an offence under subsection (1) or (2) is liable on summary conviction to a fine of an amount not exceeding level 3 on the standard scale.

INTERPRETATION
In each case a fine is related to the standard scale, so that any increases in the scale will automatically apply to offences against this Act.

COMMENT
Summary conviction may be in the Magistrates Court, so that retribution of any wrongdoing is likely to arrive fairly quickly.

17. Any sum payable in pursuance of this Act (otherwise than by way of fine) shall be recoverable summarily as a civil debt.

INTERPRETATION
If a building owner is due to make any payment to an adjoining owner (under s.11(8), for example) or fees to an adjoining owner's surveyor, and fails to do so, the injured party may produce the appropriate award to the Magistrates Court, who will order payment, with the usual sanctions. The same is true of sums due from an adjoining owner to a building owner.

COMMENT
The award will normally be adequate prima facie evidence that the sums in question are due.

18. -(1) This Act shall not apply to land which is situated in inner London and in which there is an interest belonging to –

    (a) the Honourable Society of the Inner Temple,
    (b) the Honourable Society of the Middle Temple,
    (c) the Honourable Society of Lincoln's Inn, or
    (d) the Honourable Society of Gray's Inn

(2) The reference in subsection (1) to inner London is to Greater London other than the outer London boroughs.

INTERPRETATION
Property of the Inns of Court within inner London is exempt, because it was already exempt under the former London Building Acts. Any property which they may own outside inner London is subject to this Act.

Subsection (2) defines Inner London (where there aforementioned Acts applied) because the old LCC area (which is inner London) is not formally defined anywhere.

COMMENT
It is advisable to serve notice upon the exempted parties referred to in s.18 when they are an adjoining owner.

19. - (1) This Act shall apply to land in which there is –

(a) an interest belonging to Her Majesty in right of the Crown,

(b) an interest belonging to a government department, or

(c) an interest held in trust for Her Majesty for the purposes of any such department.

(2) This Act shall apply to –

(a) land which is vested in, but not occupied by, Her Majesty in right of the Duchy of Lancaster;

(b) land which is vested in, but not occupied by, the possessor for the time being of the Duchy of Cornwall.

INTERPRETATION
The Crown is bound by this Act, except where the property is actually occupied by Her Majesty in right of the Duchy of Lancaster, or by the possessor of the Duchy of Cornwall, respectively.

COMMENT
Foreign Embassies and Ambassador's residences are considered to be foreign soil and therefore exempt from UK legislation. Nonetheless a building owner would be advised to serve notice and follow the procedures of the Act, notwithstanding this may result in an award that cannot be enforced.

s.20 : adjoining owner/adjoining occupier

20. In this Act, unless the context otherwise requires, the following expressions have the meanings hereby respectively assigned to them –

> "adjoining owner" and "adjoining occupier" respectively mean any owner and any occupier of land, buildings, storeys or rooms adjoining those of the building owner and for the purposes only of section 6 within the distances specified in that section;

INTERPRETATION

This section defines important terms used in the Act. Some are self explanatory, but they are all listed below.

When considering the terms "adjoining owner" and "adjoining occupier", particularly note that for the reasons set out in the notice to s.6(4) "adjoining" means not only "immediately adjacent to" but also, when appropriate, "within three metres" or "within six metres".

The word "any" indicates that there may well be more than one person concerned, and see the definition of "owner" below.

COMMENT
The question is often asked about the bicycle shed against the large block of flats: how many flats adjoin the shed? Received opinion is that you should serve a party structure notice on the immediately abutting property, possibly on all those directly above or below if it is likely that this work will affect them, but not on those remote to either side of the affected area.

s.20 : adjoining owner/adjoining occupier
(continued)

However, when serving a notice under s.6 against a block of flats, notice should be given to everyone for the full height of the adjacent building, within 3 or 6 metres horizontally from the excavations.

"appointing officer" means the person appointed under this Act by the local authority to make such appointments as are required under section 10(8);

INTERPRETATION
When the two surveyors cannot agree upon selecting a third surveyor, they have recourse to the local authority, meaning the authority responsible for Building Regulation control. Someone appointed by that authority makes the selection.

COMMENT
The appointing officer is normally the senior Building Control Officer.

s.20 : building owner

"building owner" means an owner of land who is desirous of exercising rights under this Act;

INTERPRETATION

The building owner is the person who initiates the work, and causes notice to be served. He must be an owner within the meaning of the Act and he cannot divest himself of responsibility under the Act by attempting to put the burden on to his contractor or insurer.

COMMENT

This is a precise term. Care should be taken to ensure that the name of the actual person or company "owning" the land and intending to carry out the work is known and given on notices and awards. Very often, large groups are a little careless in this regard, and the surveyors learn too late that a hitherto unknown subsidiary company is the legal owner.

"foundation", in relation to a wall, means the solid ground or artificially formed support resting on solid ground on which the wall rests;

INTERPRETATION

In modern terms, a foundation is usually concrete in some form: raft, beam or pile. However, when cutting off foundations under s.2(2)(g) or (h) one is likely to be dealing with spread brick footings. Foundations are what they say they are, and do not include any part of the structure further up the building, even it is takes load.

"owner" includes:

(a) a person in receipt of, or entitled to receive, the whole or part of the rents or profits of land;

(b) a person in possession of land, otherwise than as a mortgagee or as a tenant from year to year or for a lesser term or as a tenant at will;

(c) a purchaser of an interest in land under a contract for purchase or under an agreement for a lease, otherwise than under an agreement for a tenancy from year to year or for a lesser term;

INTERPRETATION
The title of owner may include more than one person in respect of the same building. There may be a freeholder, long leaseholder, tenant and sub-tenant in the same premises, all holding for a term greater than year to year. When they are "adjoining owners" they are all entitled to notice. The "building owner" is only one interest in the property where work is taking place, but his interest may be that of a purchaser under contract. He will often wish to start work as soon as possible and so has a right to serve notice as soon as he is under contract.

COMMENT
One must consider carefully the effect of changes of ownership during party wall procedures. In the case of the adjoining owner, the situation is quite clear: any incoming owner, whether acquiring from or holding under the previous owner, is bound by any notice served, appointment made, or award concluded at that date.

It is the duty of the owner who received the notice, etc to tell any incoming owner about the proceedings under the Act. The new owner also receives any benefit. As long as he served upon the person who was the adjoining owner at the date of the notice, the building owner has fulfilled his duty, and is under no obligation to serve on any new owner.

In the case of a change of building owner the situation is more complicated. It is quite clear that the building owner cannot divest himself of this responsibility by selling the property (see Selby -v- Whitbread 1917). Even if the burden runs with the land, however, it does not follow that the benefit does. It would seem that it does not, because "the building owner" is the person who must serve notice under s.3 or s.6. If he changes, then the notice he served no longer has any validity. Even an internal movement of ownership between companies in the same group produces a new owner. A new owner must serve a new notice.

Nevertheless, it will often be in the adjoining owner's interest to proceed as if there has been no change. He will probably not want a hiatus in the carrying out of the works, and would prefer to see them completed as quickly as possible. If so he will agree to waive any period of notice and appoint the same surveyor to ensure continuity. However, it would appear that if he insists upon notice running its full time, he is entitled to do so. He may also wish to ask for security for expenses from a different owner.

Contribution to the upkeep of a property through a service charge arrangement does not make someone an "owner" under the Act.

s.20 : party fence wall

"party fence wall" means a wall (not being part of a building) which stands on lands of different owners and is used or constructed to be used for separating such adjoining lands, but does not include a wall constructed on the land of one owner the artificially formed support of which projects into the land of another owner;

INTERPRETATION
In common parlance a party fence wall is a wall, such as a garden wall, astride the boundary. It does not include any wall which forms part of a building, nor a wall which only the foundations project on to the neighbouring land. See diagram opposite.

Timber fences and chain link fences are not "party fence walls" as defined by the Act.

COMMENT
Although the top right diagram has only garden on one side, it is not a party fence wall, but a party wall. The bottom diagram shows a wall belonging wholly to one owner, so it is not a party fence wall, but a boundary wall.

Party fence wall diagram

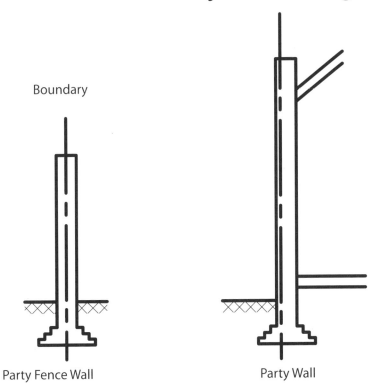

Boundary

Party Fence Wall

Party Wall

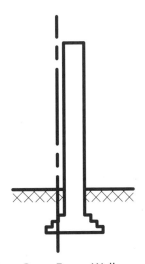

Not a Party Fence Wall

s.20 : party structure

"party structure" means a party wall and also a floor partition or other structure separating buildings or parts of buildings approached solely by separate staircases or separate entrances;

INTERPRETATION
"Party structure" is a generic term but is defined specifically to include also the floors and ceilings between any units of occupation with separate entrances. Maisonettes, flats in purpose-built blocks, and those in converted houses, will all have party structures with the premises above and/or below them, as will offices which have their own internal or external entrances. Separate entrances would mean separate doors off common hallways or lobbies.

COMMENT
Some structures are not buildings: for example, a tunnel or a bridge. A soil embankment is neither a structure nor a building.

The floor (or ceiling) of a flat is shown in the diagram and is a party structure. The same is true of blocks of self-contained offices.

Party structure diagram

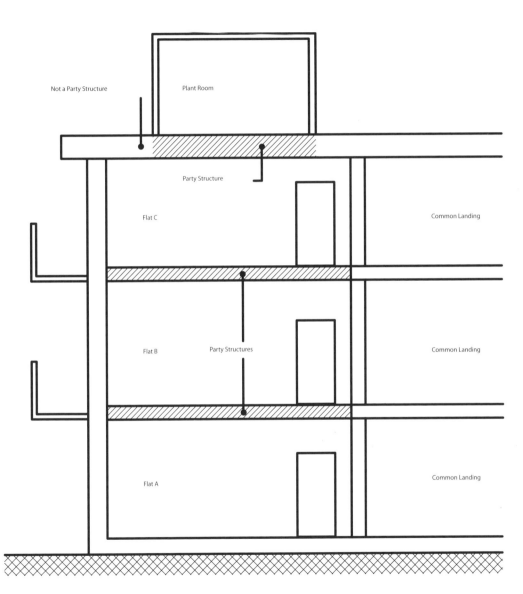

Not a Party Structure

Plant Room

Party Structure

Flat C

Common Landing

Party Structures

Flat B

Common Landing

Flat A

Common Landing

s.20 party wall (a)

"party wall" means –

(a) a wall which forms part of a building and stands on lands of different owners to a greater extent than the projection of any artificially formed support on which the wall rests; and

INTERPRETATION
"Party wall" has two definitions. In (a), as shown in the diagram opposite, it is defined as a wall which stands astride the boundary, not necessarily centrally, and not just with its footings on next door's land.

COMMENT
A party wall which stands on the land of two owners is a party wall throughout its length and height and, subject to s.2 and s.11, either owner has the right to make use of the whole of it.

Party Wall definition (a) diagram

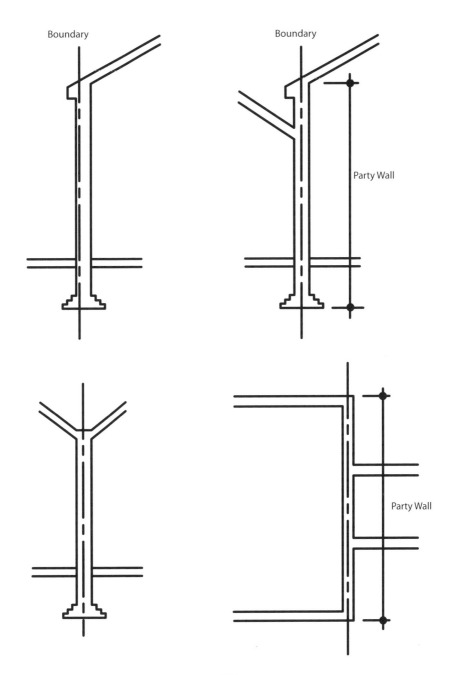

s.20 party wall (b)

["party wall" means -]

(b) so much of a wall not being a wall referred to in paragraph
     (a) above as separates buildings belonging to different
     owners;

INTERPRETATION
**In paragraph (b) it means a wall which separates the
buildings of two owners, but only that part of the wall
which actually separates the buildings of two owners is
party.**

COMMENT
*Party rights under (b) only extend as far as the enclosure by
the non-owner. He has no right to use upward or sideways
extensions of the wall, as shown in the diagrams opposite.*

*If an adjoining owner erects a building using his neighbour's
boundary wall as an enclosure, it does not become a party
wall if the neighbour had no building against it.*

*Since a wall is defined as "party" under paragraph (b) when
it separates buildings, it becomes so as soon as the second
building is placed against it, and there appears to be no
defined period for acquisition of party wall rights. It may be
that those rights are acquired immediately, but the owner of
the wall may nevertheless be able to force the
discontinuance of the unauthorised use by an injunction to
remove the trespass.*

Party wall definition (b) diagram

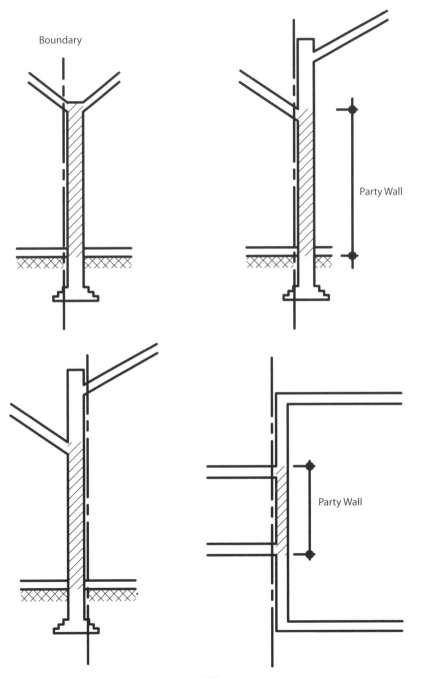

Boundary

Party Wall

Party Wall

s.20 special foundations

"special foundations" means foundations in which an assemblage of beams or rods is employed for the purpose of distributing any load; and

INTERPRETATION
"Special" means that reinforcing is used, which often creates complex foundations relying on integrity for strength, and therefore express consent is needed for their use, under s. 7(4), and specific provisions apply under s.11(10) to expenses arising from their installation.

COMMENT
They key words are "distributing any load". If a lightweight mesh is employed which can readily be cut without affecting the integrity of the foundation, it is not "special".

This means that if there is any reinforcement in any part of the foundation, the whole foundation is still "special".

Similarly, dowels used to provide a key between adjacent pins in mass concrete underpinning does not make it a "special foundation".

"surveyor" means any person not being a party to the matter appointed or selected under section 10 to determine disputes in accordance with the procedures set out in this Act.

INTERPRETATION

An owner may not nominate himself as his surveyor, but he may choose anyone else. It is obviously highly desirable, however, that he should appoint someone experienced in the kind of work involved, such as a building surveyor, architect or engineer, and preferably one with a specialist knowledge of the procedures to be followed under this Act.

COMMENT

An employee of an owner who does not have a financial interest in that owner's company could be appointed as surveyor but he must feel able to act impartially and independently without influence from his employer (the owner).

Similarly, an employee of a local authority can be appointed as the surveyor under the Act but must be prepared to act impartially of other responsibilities that pertain to that employment.

21. - (1)   The Secretary of State may by order amend or repeal any provision of a private or local Act passed before or in the same session as this Act, if it appears to him necessary or expedient to do so in consequence of this Act.

(2)   An order under subsection (1) may –

(a)   contain such savings or transitional provisions as the Secretary of State thinks fit;

(b)   make different provision for different purposes.

(3)   The power to make an order under subsection (1) shall be exercisable by statutory instrument subject to annulment in pursuance of a resolution of either House of Parliament.

General

22. - (1) This Act may be cited as the Party Wall etc Act 1996.

(2) This Act shall come into force in accordance with provision made by the Secretary of State by order made by statutory instrument.

(3) An order under subsection (2) may –

    (a)   contain such savings or transitional provisions as the Secretary of State thinks fit;

    (b)   make different provision for different purposes.

(4) This Act extends to England and Wales only.

APPENDIX

Specimen Documents

There are no special forms required to be used under the Act, but we have set out some suggested models in the pages that follow. These may be photocopied for use, but it will be necessary carefully to delete or to insert the right names, paragraphs, etc., if the forms are to be correct. Leading cases under earlier Acts have held that if the Notice does not adequately identify the clauses of the act under which work is proposed, or clearly state what that work is, then the requirements of the Act have not been fulfilled.

It is a mistake to think that all will be well if every lettered paragraph is left in- on the contrary, the result will be an unenforceable ambiguity. The relevant paragraphs must be carefully selected and all others deleted.

The draft award given here is an example of one made by two surveyors. It can readily be adapted for use by a Third Surveyor, an agreed surveyor, or a surveyor acting ex parte. This is provided for guidance only and must be reviewed specifically for every individual matter.

Appendix

Suggested Letters of Appointment of Surveyors

1. Appointment of Building Owner's/s' Surveyor

Dear

re: [address of Building Owner's/s' property] and the Party Wall etc. Act 1996

You are hereby authorised to sign, serve and receive any notices in connection with the works proposed at the above address. In the event of a dispute arising we appoint you, in accordance with section 10 of the Act as my/our Surveyor. I/we also authorise you to make any necessary appointments under that section on our behalf.

Yours etc.

2. Appointment of Adjoining Owner's/s' Surveyor

Dear

re: [address of Adjoining Owner's/s' property] and the Party Wall etc. Act 1996

In connection with the Notice dated   served on   me/us under the above Act, I/we hereby appoint you,   , in accordance with section 10 of the Act as my/our Surveyor.

Yours etc,

Party Wall etc. Act 1996
LINE OF JUNCTION NOTICE

To:

of:

as Adjoining Owner/s under the Act of the premises known as:

I/We:

of:

as Building Owner/s under the Act of:

which adjoins your premises

HEREBY SERVE YOU WITH NOTICE
under section 1(2),

that if you consent in writing it is intended to build on the line of junction of the said premises a party wall/ party fence wall

under section 1(5),

that it is intended at my/our own expense to build on the line of junction of the said premises a wall wholly on my/our own land and will/will not place projecting footings and foundations below the level of your land under section 1(6)

under section 7(4),

that with your written consent, it is proposed to use special foundations.

The proposed works as shown on the accompanying drawings are:

It is intended to commence works after one month or earlier by agreement. Where any dispute arises under section 1 (8), section 10 of the Act requires that both parties should concur in the appointment of a Surveyor, or should each appoint one Surveyor, and in those circumstances I/we would appoint as my/our Surveyor:

of:

SIGNED:

Authorised to sign on behalf of: (Building Owner/s)
DATE:

Party Wall etc. Act 1996

PARTY NOTICE STRUCTURE

To:

of:

as Adjoining Owner/s under the Act of the premises known as:

I/We:

of:

as Building Owner/s under the Act of:

which adjoins your premises
HEREBY SERVE YOU WITH NOTICE
THAT IN ACCORDANCE WITH/OUR RIGHTS
under section 2 subsection (2) (a) (b) (c) (d) (e) (f) (g) (h) (i) (j) (k) (l) (m) (n) and with reference to the PARTY STRUCTURE/PARTY WALL/PARTY FENCE WALL separating the above premises, it is intended to carry out the works detailed below, after the expiration of two months from service of this Notice.

The proposed works are:

It is intended to commence works when notice has run or earlier by agreement.

Under section 5, if you do not consent to the works within 14 days you are deemed to have dissented and a dispute is deemed to have arisen. In that case section 10 of the Act requires that both parties should concur in the appointment of a Surveyor, or should each appoint one Surveyor, and in those circumstances I/we would appoint:

of:

SIGNED:

authorised to sign on behalf of: (Building Owner/s)

DATE:

Party Wall etc. Act 1996

ACKNOWLEDGEMENT OF PARTY STRUCTURE NOTICE

I/We:

of:

as Adjoining Owner/s under the Act of the premises known as:

having received the Notice served by:

of:

in respect of:

which adjoins my/our premises, and in relation to the works proposed under section 2 subsection (2), paragraphs:

hereby CONSENT to the proposed works
or
hereby DISSENT from the above works and, a dispute having arisen, concur in the appointment of/appoint as a Surveyor:

of:

SIGNED:

authorised to sign on behalf of: (Adjoining Owner/s)

DATE:

Party Wall etc. Act 1996

THREE METRE/SIX METRE NOTICE

To:

of:

as Adjoining Owner/s under the Act of the premises known as:

I/We:

of:

as Building Owner/s under the Act

which adjoins your premises

HEREBY SERVE YOU WITH NOTICE
THAT IN ACCORDANCE MY/OUR RIGHTS

under section 6(1) it is intended to build within 3 metres of your building and to a lower level than the bottom of your foundations, by carrying out the works detailed below, after the expiration of one month from the service of this Notice.

Or

under section 6(2) it is intended to build within 6 metres of your building and to a depth as defined in the Act, by carrying out the works detailed below, after the expiration of one month from the service of this Notice.

IT IS/IS NOT PROPOSED TO UNDERPIN OR OTHERWISE
STRENGTHEN OR SAFEGUARD THE FOUNDATIONS OF YOUR
BUILDING.

The accompanying plans and sections show the site and the excavation depth proposed. The intended works are:

It is intended to commence works when notice has run or earlier by agreement. Under section 6(7), if you do not consent to the works within 14 days you are deemed to have dissented and a dispute is deemed to have arisen. In that case section 10 of the Act requires that both parties should concur in the appointment of a Surveyor or should each appoint one Surveyor and in those circumstances I/we would appoint:

Of:

SIGNED:

authorised to sign on behalf of: (Building Owner/s)

DATE:

Party Wall etc. Act 1996

ACKNOWLEDGEMENT OF THREE METRE/SIX METRE NOTICE

I/We:

of:

as Adjoining Owner/s under the Act of the premises known as:

having received the Notice served by:

of:

in respect of:

which adjoins my/our premises,

      hereby CONSENT to the proposed works

      or

      require you to underpin or strengthen or safeguard the foundations of my/our building

      or

      dispute the necessity for underpinning or strengthening or safeguarding the foundations of my/our building

and a dispute having arisen concur in the appointment of/appoint as a Surveyor:

of:

SIGNED:

authorised to sign on behalf of: (Adjoining Owner/s)

DATE:

AN AWARD under the provisions of the PARTY WALL etc ACT 1996 to be published to the Appointing owners under section 10(140

Whereas *[the Building Owner/s]*
of
(hereinafter referred to as the Building Owner/s) an owner/s within the meaning of the said Act of the premises known as

did on the   day of   Two Thousand and
serve upon [the Adjoining owner/s]
of
(hereinafter referred to as the Adjoining Owner/s) freehold/leasehold owner/s within the meaning of the Act of the adjoining premises know as
Notice of his/their intention to exercise the rights given to him/them by the Party Wall etc. Act 1996 section (s) 1,2 2(a) (b) (c) (d) (e) (f) (g) (h) (i) (j) (k) (l) (m) (n) and 6 (1) (2) by executing works as more particularly defined in the Notice.

AND WHEREAS the Building Owner/s has/have appointed

of
to act as his/their Surveyor and the Adjoining Owner/s has/have appointed
of
to act as his/their Surveyor.

AND WHEREAS the two Surveyors so appointed have selected
of
to act as Third Surveyor in accordance with the provisions of the Act and, in the event of his being unable or unwilling to act and their being unable jointly to agree upon a substitute, they have agreed that another Third Surveyor shall be selected by the appointing officer of the Local Authority in accordance with the section 10 (8) of the Act.

NOW WE, being two of the three Surveyors so appointed and the said premises having been inspected DO HEREBY AWARD AND DETERMINE as follows:

1 (a) That the wall separating the Building and Adjoining Owner's/s premises is deemed to be a party wall/party fence wall within the meaning of the Act.

(b) That *[the Adjoining Owner's/s building]*
stands close to or adjoins the Building Owner's/s premises within the meaning of the Act.

(c) That the Schedule of Condition dated
attached hereto and signed by us the said two Surveyors forms part of this Award.

(d) That the said party wall/party fence wall as described in the attached Schedule of Condition is sufficient for the present purposes of the Adjoining Owner/s.

(e) That drawing/s No./s
attached hereto and signed by us the said two Surveyors form/s part of this Award.

2.	That after the service of the signed Award the Building Owner/s shall be at liberty if he/they so choose/s, but shall be under no obligation to carry out the following works:

3.	That no deviation from the agreed works shall be made without the prior consultation with and agreement between the owners or in the event of a dispute, by the appointed surveyors in accordance with section 10 of the Act.

4.	That if the Building Owner/s exercise/s the above rights he/they shall:

(a) Execute the whole of the aforesaid works at the sole cost of the Building Owner/s.

(b) Take all reasonable precautions and provide all necessary support to retain the Adjoining Owner's/s' land and buildings.

(c) Make good all damage to the Adjoining Owner's/s building occasioned by the said works where so required by the Act in materials to match existing works to the satisfaction of the appointed Surveyors, or if so required by the Adjoining Owner/s make payment in lieu of carrying out the work to make the damage good.

(d) Hold the Adjoining Owner/s free from liability for any injury or loss of life to any person or damage to property caused by, or in consequence of, the execution of the said works.

(e) Bear the costs of the making of any justified claims.

(f) Permit the Adjoining Owner's/s Surveyor to have access to the Building Owner's/s premises at all reasonable times during the progress of the said works.

(g) Carry out the whole of the said works so far as practicable from the Building Owner's/s side. Where access to the Adjoining Owner's/s premises is required reasonable notice shall be given in accordance with section 8 of the Act.

(h) Remove any scaffolding or screens as soon as possible and clear away dust and debris from time to time as necessary.

5. That the Building Owner's/s Surveyor shall be permitted access to the Adjoining Owner's/s property from time to time during the progress of the works at reasonable times and after giving reasonable notice.

6. That the whole of the works referred to in this Award shall be executed in accordance with Building Regulations, and any other requirements of statutory authorities, and shall be executed in a proper and workmanlike manner in sound and suitable materials in accordance with the terms of this Award to the reasonable satisfaction of the Adjoining Owner's/s Surveyor.

7. That the works shall be carried through with reasonable expedition after commencement and so as to avoid any unnecessary inconvenience to the Adjoining Owner/s or occupier/s.

In particular, noisy works the subject of this Award shall be restricted to between the hours of
and   excepting   weekends   and Bank Holidays when no works shall be executed.

8.   That the signed Awards shall be served on the Appointing Owners forthwith. An unsigned copy of the documents shall also be provided for the Adjoining Owner's/s Surveyor.

9.   That upon the signing of this Award the Building Owner/s shall pay the Adjoining Owner's/s Surveyors fee of £   plus   VAT   in   connection   with   the preparation   of   this   Award   and   [*insert   number*] subsequent inspections of the works. In the event of damage being caused or other contingencies or variations arising, a further fee shall be payable.

10.   That the Surveyors reserve the right to make and issue any further Award or Awards that may be necessary, as provided in the said Act.

11.   That this Award shall be null and void if the permitted works do not commence within 12 months from the date of this Award.

12.   Nothing in this Award shall be held as conferring, admitting or affecting any right of light or easement in or relating to a party wall.

IN WITNESS WHEREOF we have set our hands

Day of   Two Thousand and

Surveyor to the Building Owner/s:

Witness:

Occupation:

Address:

Surveyor to the Adjoining Owner/s:

Witness:

Occupation:

Address:

INDEX OF KEY TERMS

Words which occur in almost every clause have not been indexed, but others which the reader may wish to find have been listed.

154

INDEX OF KEY TERMS

INDEX OF KEY TERMS

INDEX OF KEY TERMS

Notes

Notes

me of junchi

S. 1(1)(a)
~~8a~~ d(b)

S. 1. (6)(a) ~~&~~ b

S. 2(2)(a)
~~S. 2(2)~~
S 2(2)(f)
S. 2(2)(g)   S 2(2)(j)
S 2(2)(k)
S 2(2)(l)
S. 2 (2)(n)

S. 6(1)(a) ~~&b~~

S 6(3)

S 6(6)(a) ~~&~~(b)

Notes